SPIRITUALLY MATURE YOGA

Christopher Sartain

ISBN: 1517756057
ISBN-13: 978-1517756055

DEDICATION

I dedicate this book to the Spiritual Masters of the Kriya Yoga tradition: Babaji, Lahiri Mahasaya, Sri Yukteswar, Paramahansa Yogananda, and Roy Eugene Davis.

CONTENTS

ACKNOWLEDGMENTS

I acknowledge the constant inspiration of the Divine presence found in Nature. The majestic beauty of the Southern Andes Mountains was integral in the completion of this work. I also acknowledge the love and support of my wife, Carolina.

1 INTRODUCTION

"By assuming personal responsibility for the choices we make and the actions we perform, we can actualize psychological health and emotional maturity necessary for well-being and spiritual growth."
-Roy Eugene Davis

Yoga is a term, a concept, and a reality that has been misunderstood and misrepresented in the West. I believe that yogis in the West have a duty to uphold the sacred meaning of Yoga, as it continues to lose more and more of its original intent and purpose. The consumer culture of the Western world has transformed Yoga into a business and a fashion trend, and many of the Spiritual aspects and practices of Yoga have been replaced by skin-tight yoga pants and electronic "smart mats". Much of our treatment of Yoga here in the West has to do with the fact that we are a Spiritually immature culture as a whole. The Spiritual sanctity of Yoga has been sullied due to this Spiritual immaturity, and it is my sincere hope that this book might serve as a wakeup call to many in the West who consider themselves "yogis."

The Westernization of Yoga has also been beneficial for Yoga as a whole. For example, Western Yoga has largely stripped away the Guru and deity worship, as well as the unnecessary ritual aspects, of Indian Yoga. Due to the secular nature of Western Yoga, we have collectively realized the arbitrary nature of deity worship, complicated fire ceremonies, unscientific belief systems, superstitious mythology, and other non-essential practices and customs. However, with this "trimming of the religious fat" comes the unintended consequence of a taking Yoga completely out of its Spiritual context. Yoga is, at its core, a Spiritual practice.

There is a misunderstanding and confusion in the West that regards religion and Spirituality as the same thing. This has led to the removal of both the religious and Spiritual components of Yoga, mistakenly understood to be equal. When Paramahansa Yogananda first introduced Yoga to the West, it was presented in its Spiritual and scientific context, but this understanding of Yoga has drastically changed in the time since Yogananda's passing in 1952. While the removal of Indian religious beliefs has been good for Yoga overall, the removal of the Spirituality of Yoga to appease those Westerners still clinging to a Judeo-Christian belief system has been detrimental to our understanding of Yoga.

I would like to dispel early on any notion that attending a weekly asana class at the local gym or "Yoga" studio qualifies as the sole requisite for consideration as a yogi. Yoga is not mere asana. What most uneducated people consider to be Yoga is actually a modernized form of Hatha Yoga combined with European Gymnastics that has only existed for about one hundred years.

I have heard the term yogi bandied about and misused so often that I am not sure we ever had a true sense of the characteristics of a true yogi in the West. However, perhaps it is time we reviewed the matter. A yogi, by definition, is one who practices Yoga. Yoga, in the Yoga Sutras of Patanjali, is synonymous with the word Samadhi and they are used interchangeably. Since the Yoga Sutras is the most famous and authoritative treatise on Yoga, it seems appropriate that we should use the definition given therein. In order to be considered a yogi, one must be sincerely attempting to experience Samadhi on a regular basis via their Yoga and meditation practices. In fact, until one has experienced Samadhi, Yoga cannot even be understood or known due to the simple fact that Yoga is Samadhi. I used to think that Samadhi was somehow the end of the Spiritual journey, but I realize now that it is where the true Spiritual journey actually begins.

Samadhi is the union of one's attention and awareness with the Infinite. For consideration as a true yogi, one should be engaged in consistent daily practices working towards the attainment of Samadhi or Divine Union. Attending a "hot core power flow" class once a week and posting a few selfies of fancy postures on social media will not result in Enlightenment, which is the ultimate goal of Yoga practice. One must be engaged in a regular, deep meditation practice to experience the Oneness Consciousness that is unveiled during profound Samadhi states.

Another way of defining Yoga according to Patanjali comes from the second verse; Yoga chitta vritti nirodha. When translated correctly from the original Sanskrit, this Sutra means that Yoga is experienced when the fluctuations in our Being cease. When all the waves, fluctuations, or vibrations happening within us cease, Yoga (Union) is what remains. These fluctuations include thoughts, emotions, desires, memories, physical sensations, etc...All of these fluctuations keep our awareness identified with our false self consisting of the body-mind-personality composite. When we are able to experience Yoga/Samadhi, our awareness is no longer identified with the temporary, finite self and the truth of what we are is unveiled, Pure Infinite Consciousness. There is no sense of separation during Samadhi, there is only a Oneness and wholeness beyond description.

In the West, Yoga has been equated with asana. Asana, as defined by Patanjali, is a comfortable seated posture for meditation and nothing more. However, over time, yogis created many asanas for the purposes of preparing the body for meditation and these were recorded in the texts of Hatha Yoga between five hundred and three hundred years ago approximately. The Hatha Yoga Pradipika, Shiva Samhita, and Gheranda Samhita list dozens of postures or asanas. However, modern yogis might be surprised to learn that far more importance was given to pranayama, meditation, mantras, bandhas, mudras, and hygiene than was given to asana in these classic texts. Therefore, even one who would argue that people practicing solely asana could be considered yogis because they are practicing Hatha Yoga, which is a form of Yoga, would be mistaken. I have been to so called "Hatha Yoga" classes only to find instructors leading students through a shallow asana class, with no pranayamas, mantras, mudras, bandhas, or meditations, which are the focus of Hatha. The goal of Hatha is still Samadhi and Self-Realization, and the practice of asana was simply meant as preparation for meditation, and not preparation for looking good in a pair of yoga pants (the modern goal).

In each chapter I will be giving examples of how we might move from a state of Spiritual immaturity into a state of Spiritual maturity. At times throughout the text I will be using the terms emotional maturity and Spiritual maturity interchangeably depending on the context. Spiritual maturity may be defined as one's ability or capacity to live in a responsible and wise manner and emotional maturity may be defined as one's ability or capacity to respond to situations in an appropriate and responsible manner.

I was at a weeklong meditation retreat at Center for Spiritual Awareness in North Georgia in 2009 when someone gave me some truly sage advice regarding Spiritual maturity. I have always suffered from poison ivy allergies, and I was dealing with a fairly serious episode during the retreat. I walked by one of the retreat participants, who has since become a friend of mine, and he saw me scratching my forearm where the rash was at its worst. He commented on my affliction and I responded by telling him of my love for nature and how I have trouble staying out of the woods in the summer time and how it was all my own fault for getting the rash. After I admitted that the rash was my fault, he responded by saying, "Everything is." This has continued to resonate in the very core of my Being ever since and it truly awakened me to the reasons and causes behind the circumstances in my life, both good and bad. What a realization is was to comprehend the cause and effect relationship of karma and my central role in it all!

Shortly after this realization, I stopped playing the blame game that had taken up the better part of my adult life and began to take responsibility for my own actions and circumstances. Most people wander aimlessly through life blaming others and the world for their problems and never take responsibility for their actions and choices. They would rather make excuses instead of making positive changes in their lives that would improve their circumstances. If we are experiencing a bad mood, a negative attitude, or emotional suffering, it is because we have chosen that experience. This book is, in reality, nothing more than a grand elaboration upon that one simple, yet profound statement, "Everything is your fault."

I would also like to assure the reader that I write from my own personal experience having dealt with extreme levels of Spiritual and emotional immaturity in my past. Every situation and example given in this book is something that I, myself, have had to deal with and transcend at one point or another. I do not write of overcoming Spiritual immaturity from some holier than thou, judgmental point of reference, but rather from a sense of empathy and compassion for my fellow yogis who find themselves confronting similar situations and problems as described in the book.

Through this work, I hope to instill in the reader the importance of self responsibility and the idea that we cannot, and should not rely on anything or anyone from the outside for Spiritual growth. If there is one decisive mistake that I see people making repeatedly on the Spiritual path it is over-reliance on things such as Spiritual communities, Gurus, savior figures, drugs, and other outside means for their Spiritual unfoldment. Spiritual maturity is the realization that we are the ones ultimately responsible for our lives and our Spiritual Enlightenment.

2 SENSE PLEASURE

"Without Self-knowledge, there is no possibility of having true peace. When one's attention is allowed to dwell on objects of desire and the senses become stimulated, the mind follows, as a boat on the water is carried away by the wind. Mental restlessness then obscures Self-knowledge."
-Sri Yukteswar

A clear indication of one's level of Spiritual and emotional immaturity is their attachment to sense pleasures. A large part of the path to Spiritual maturity and Enlightenment is the transcendence of the desire for sense pleasures. When we remain attached to sense pleasures such as sex, drugs, food, television, etc...we maintain our identification with the false self that desires pleasure in one form or another. As long as we are chasing after pleasure, our consciousness will remain bound within the finite, temporary self that has no fixed or permanent reality. Complete Liberation (a stage beyond preliminary states of Enlightenment) is impossible for one who remains addicted to the world of sense pleasure. Liberation is only possible for one who has renounced entirely the desire to experience worldly pleasures and has attained a state of Infinite contentment beyond the sensory world.

For one intent on the goal of Spiritual Enlightenment, addiction is a supreme obstacle. There are many forms that addiction may take in one's life, but drug addiction is certainly the most nefarious. Many people battle with drug addiction and a large percentage never win the battle and die as addicts. What we do not defeat, we are destined to repeat. The law of karma (cause and effect) stipulates that whatever addictions we leave the world with, we must conquer in the next life.

Reincarnation is real. There is ample evidence for the transmigration of the soul that has been collected by the monks of the Tibetan tradition and many other traditions in India, and also by Ian Stevenson at the University of Virginia. I have had mystical experiences in which I have remembered myself in the "unborn" state existing in an astral realm and preparing for incarnation into form. I have vivid memories of "choosing" my current parents and sister before I was reborn. Choosing might not be the correct word; it was more like I was attracted to my family by some unseen force. I can also remember entering into the DNA molecules of the newly created zygote and wrapping my astral self around the double helix, impregnating form with my Being. I have also had innumerable experiences where people, places, and smells (oddly enough) are eerily familiar, which can only mean that I have had contact with them in previous lives. I have recognized all of the important people in my life immediately upon meeting them for the first time. Needless to say, I, along with many others, can personally attest to the reality of reincarnation.

Therefore, it is of the utmost importance that we deal with our addiction and attachment issues in this current incarnation so that we do not have to deal with them in future incarnations. Drugs adhere us to this illusory plane, and thus we remain in bondage. Until we can break the chains of drug addiction, we have no hope of Spiritual freedom. It is recommended in the Yoga tradition that we abstain from all drugs, including alcohol. The allure of certain drugs is so powerful that even one experience with them can result in lifelong addiction problems.

People often mistake maturity for one's ability to achieve success in academics, career, and finance. However, when we begin to see things from the perspective of multiple lifetimes, we quickly realize that we cannot take our college degrees, job titles, and bank accounts with us when we die. We do take with us our states of mind and consciousness and our karma/emotional baggage. Knowing this, we can reevaluate our definition of maturity as something that has far more to do with emotional and Spiritual growth and less to do with material growth and mundane matters.

In Patanjali's Yoga Sutras, we are given an ethical code to follow as yogis known as the yamas and niyamas. This set of ten rules for living, when strictly followed, can assist us greatly on our path to Spiritual maturity and Enlightenment. The yamas (restraints) are ahimsa (non-harm), satya (truthfulness), asteya (non-stealing), brahmacharya (conservation), and aparigraha (non-attachment). The niyamas (observances) are saucha (purity), santosha (contentment), tapas (discipline), svadhyaya (self-study), and ishvarapranidhana (surrender to God).

Many so called yogis are not even aware of the existence of a moral code in the philosophy of Yoga. For example, I have seen in recent days many advertisements for "Yoga and cocktails" or "Yoga and wine." With even a rudimentary understanding of the Yamas/Niyamas, such an idea is utterly absurd. How can one be expected to practice non-harm, non-attachment, purity, and contentment by imbibing a toxic substance like alcohol, especially right after a Yoga session? Take contentment for example; each time we use drugs or have a drink we are admitting to ourselves that we are not content. If we were, there would be no desire to change our condition via the use of drugs or alcohol. If people want to have an "aerobics and stretching class" and get drunk afterward, that is their business and they should be free to do so, but they should not use the word Yoga to describe what they are doing. This is a clear example of the ignorance surrounding the word Yoga and its use in the West. Offering a Yoga class followed by intoxicants is like offering a weight-loss class followed by a junk food binge. It is infantile and exhibits a complete lack of Spiritual maturity.

Yoga is a process by which we leave behind our need for sense pleasure. When we begin to experience the deep bliss or ananda of our Spiritual practices, the need for the sense pleasure offered by drugs becomes obsolete and supercilious. The problem is that it generally takes years of consistent meditation practice before one begins to experience the true bliss of superconscious states. However, once one has some experience with ananda, or the bliss of God-communion, the idea of returning to drugs is like tasting a juicy, ripe strawberry for the first time and having the desire to return to eating shriveled, moldy strawberries. The first experiences of ananda may take many months or years to experience, but these experiences are well worth the wait. The problem is that in our modern world, people expect instant gratification and they do not possess the maturity or patience to wait for the delayed gratification that Spiritual practice promises, so they prefer instead the instantaneous effects of drugs and alcohol.

One of the main issues associated with drug use is the avoidance of dealing with emotional issues or karmic baggage. When an emotional issue arises, rather than dealing with it, the drug user drinks a beer or smokes a joint instead, and the issue remains unresolved. The addict continually covers up their emotional "stuff" and they remain as a child emotionally. Anyone who has quit a drug or has been around a recovering addict knows the tribulations of the first year or two of recovery as the person in recovery finally has to deal with a life's worth of emotional baggage all at once. It is because of this sudden onslaught of karmic buildup that most addicts relapse and return to their drug of choice after a month or two. However, if someone can manage to garner the inner strength and resilience it requires to make it past the first year or so of emotional tumult, they have a much greater probability of breaking the bonds of addiction and achieving emotional freedom.

One drug that is particularly harmful for one on the Spiritual path is marijuana. I know many so called yogis that continue to use marijuana and still consider themselves to be on a Spiritual path. I have even heard some people say that marijuana "gets them closer to God." Anyone who would say something like this obviously has no experience of God and is in a state of complete Spiritual ignorance. I have personally used marijuana in my past so I have a basis for comparison as opposed to an evangelical preacher with no experience who might say something similar. The main problem with marijuana is that it is the drug of complacency. Marijuana addicts are always complacently content with wherever they are in life Spiritually and emotionally and rarely try to do much to improve their circumstances and situation. I have never met a Spiritually advanced marijuana addict and I never will because they simply do not exist. There are traditions in India where certain sects of sadhus use marijuana as a "sacrament" to Shiva, whatever that means. They remain in a state of bondage for their entire lives, and are forced to reincarnate time and again so they can satisfy their childish desire to get high and escape reality.

As one who has experience with marijuana, I can say with confidence that it is impossible to experience clear states of superconsciousness while under the influence of the drug. I can certainly understand the need for people who have chronic illnesses to use marijuana as a medicine to treat their ailment. However, the vast majority of the people who say they are using marijuana medicinally have no chronic illness. Obviously people with glaucoma, cancer, Crohn's disease, epilepsy, and the like should be free to use marijuana as a medicine and its prohibition for medicinal use is ridiculous. However, if a person is using marijuana and they are not sick, then it is not a medicine; it is a highly addictive drug that is a major obstacle on the Spiritual path. The idea that marijuana is somehow not addictive is asinine. Anyone serious about Spiritual awakening would be wise to leave marijuana behind and begin living a life of emotional and Spiritual maturity.

There is an interesting trend happening amongst certain new age groups involving the use of peyote and ayahuasca and other psychedelic drugs for Spiritual benefit. While these drugs can, in fact, be Spiritually beneficial and awaken our Kundalini (the evolutionary force of consciousness), they are entirely unnecessary. Again, I speak from direct experience and I can personally attest to the fact that these drugs can only take one so far. There are states of consciousness that go beyond what one is able to experience on a "trip." Also, I have had many "psychedelic" experiences without the use of any drugs or outside substances. In fact, to be perfectly honest, I feel like I am having a psychedelic experience almost all the time now after years of deep meditation resulting in Kundalini awakening. Kundalini is the evolutionary force of consciousness that is said to be coiled potential energy resting in a dormant state at the base of our astral spine (sushumna nadi) awaiting activation through Spiritual practice. It is often associated with serpent symbolism because it is said to be coiled like a snake wrapped around our central energetic channel or sushumna.

The main problem with the use of substances for Spiritual growth is a dependency upon the substances that results in addiction. I have known many people who participate in peyote circles several times a month, but who claim they are not addicted. Dependence upon anything outside of ourselves for Spiritual experience can only result in delusion and bondage. There is absolutely no need for the use of drugs in order to elicit Spiritual experiences. They are completely unnecessary. Some shamans that I have met are nothing more than glorified drug addicts. There are a few legitimate shamans in the Amazon and elsewhere who have miraculously cured diseases with ayahuasca and I do not discount the medicinal benefits of such drugs, but the majority of shamans are con-men interested in making a quick buck, just like many modern Yoga Gurus. It is also important to mention the over-glorification of the Amazonian shaman that is happening currently. It is important to keep in mind that many of these shamans were living in cannibalistic tribes only a few decades ago and that these are people who never invented writing, and yet so many doughy eyed followers are ready to worship them as Spiritual Masters. It is always good to see the bigger picture.

Our Being is a Divine template of awakening. We have everything within our physical, mental, and astral selves necessary for complete Spiritual Enlightenment. We did not make it through thousands of years of bio-spiritual evolution in the cosmos only to wake up one day and realize that God left something out of our composition. Our bodies are a technological miracle and we possess a nervous system and brain capable of processing incredibly high states of consciousness once the nervous system and brain have been properly and adequately prepared. The regular use of psychedelic drugs actually weakens the nervous system and leaves it in a frazzled, damaged state, whereas the practices of asana, pranayama, and meditation safely refine and purify the brain and nervous system and prepare it for higher states of consciousness and being.

In many ways, Enlightenment is a physiological process. Through the practices of asana, pranayama, chanting, and meditation we prepare the physical body to process higher vibrational states of being. This is why most people experimenting with psychedelic drugs "freak out." They have not properly prepared the brain and nervous system to process the altered state of being that occurs in the physical body during a trip. Yoga and meditation is a far safer and more mature way to enter into higher astral realms and states of consciousness.

A large part of the physiological process associated with Spiritual awakening has to do with neuroplasticity. Our brain and neural pathways are altered dramatically through a disciplined meditation practice. Meditation literally rewires the brain to have the capacity to experience superconsciousness and Samadhi. Each time we meditate superconsciously, we short circuit the messages that the body sends to the brain about sense pleasures and our incessant need for them. Yoga and meditation can be thought of as the intentional rewiring of the brain to accommodate higher states of consciousness. The brain and nervous system is like a high-tech Spiritual antenna, and through our practices we fine tune the antenna to receive transmissions from the Divine.

The hallucinations and visions that can be perceived during a psychedelic trip are still a part of the illusory world of maya, a Sanskrit word that means illusion. Because the world is in constant motion and impermanent, it is ultimately an illusion. The only "thing" that is real is Infinite Consciousness. Therefore, the psychedelic experience is nothing more than an illusion within the illusion. It is no more real than the world and mind in which it takes place. It has been my experience that people who participate in peyote and ayahuasca ceremonies do so primarily because they are interested in Spiritual entertainment.

There are many forms of Spiritual entertainment available to seekers in today's modern Spiritual landscape. With regards to Spiritual entertainment, my Guru, Roy Eugene Davis, says, "I know people who frequently attend lectures or seminars presented by almost every new age teacher, yogi, shaman, or 'quick enlightenment' promoter who visits their community without demonstrating obvious benefits." Likewise, I know of many "Spiritual shoppers" who have been to many workshops dealing with sacred geometry, astral projection, chakra balancing, the law of attraction, quantum physics, energy healing, channeling, automatic writing, past-life recall, hypnosis, astrology, remote viewing, spirit guides, herbalism, and a variety of others, and they are no better off than they were before they attended the workshops. Many of them have disordered lives, dysfunctional relationships, addiction problems, deep emotional issues, and delusional belief systems. Workshops such as the ones mentioned above are very entertaining, but they are not transformational and they do not result is higher states of consciousness. Personally, I have attended similar workshops only to find that I have more stuff in my head, but that nothing Spiritually beneficial was actually gained. There is certainly nothing wrong with a little Spiritual shopping and Spiritual entertainment early on, but once we find the path of superconscious meditation, things like peyote ceremonies and tarot card readings become arbitrary and irrelevant.

The psychedelic drug experience is just one more way to indulge the senses in a futile attempt to fill an insatiable void within. The false self is never content, and will continue its pursuance of sense pleasures in a never ending cycle of temporary satisfaction followed by disappointment and craving. It is this craving that disturbs our inner peace and creates vrittis or fluctuations in our Being that prevent stillness and Yoga from occurring. Yoga is impossible to experience when there is constant craving and desire. The continued pursuit of sense pleasures while engaging in Spiritual practice is akin to hiking up a snowy mountain taking one step forward only to slip back two steps on the path with each stride.

Possibly the strongest of human cravings is that of the sexual urge. In fact, many yogis and Masters say that it is the last urge to go after one has conquered cravings for drugs and food and all other sense pleasures. This certainly seems to be the case and sex is considered a basic biological human function like eating, drinking, evacuation, and sleeping. It is for this very reason that many truth teachers recommend maintaining a regulated sexual life with a devoted partner. What is not recommended is an undisciplined life full of promiscuity resulting in restlessness and emotional confusion. Marriage and monogamy is by far the most emotionally and Spiritually mature option available to us as yogis. If we are blessed enough to find a compatible life partner, then we should remain committed to that one person for life, and it is absolutely possible to have a satisfying sex life and continue on a Spiritual Enlightenment path. One need not give up their sex life completely to experience higher states of consciousness. However, especially for yogis, it is important to conserve sexual energy through the practice of Brahmacharya.

Ancient Ayurvedic texts recommend that partners should only engage in the sexual act every two weeks, or twice a month. This is due to complicated theories regarding the production of a subtle energetic substance known as ojas. This ojas is produced by, or is at least associated with, the sexual fluids of men and women. Ojas gives a yogi his or her radiance and it is important not to deplete ojas so that we may maintain optimum health and vitality. It is said that it takes about two weeks to reproduce ojas following ejaculation and so men in particular should allow for two weeks time in between ejaculations. The Tantric yogis found ways around this by using a little known method to have an orgasm without ejaculating, but needless to say, we should do our best to conserve our vital energies and regulate our sexual activity.

There are also those yogis who prefer a life of celibacy and monastic renunciation. There is nothing wrong with this choice, but most of the people that I have met in this situation love nothing more than to boast about how long they have been celibate and why a life of renunciation is far superior to a householder life. Also, celibacy more often than not leads to issues associated with sexual repression, and in many instances, child molestation and pedophilia like in the case of Catholic priests and monks.

Furthermore, sexual perversion of any kind is to be avoided along with the use of pornography, which leads to unrealistic fantasies and sexual cravings. Pornography is a pernicious plague affecting people the world over. The brain is quickly rewired after just a few experiences with pornography and addiction is incredibly difficult to overcome. A majority of men in the United States report viewing porn on a weekly basis. There are also new reports that around one third of women view porn regularly now as well in the US. For yogis serious about Spiritual Enlightenment, the use of pornography is to be avoided due to its capacity to rewire the brain and cause serious addiction problems. However, if one is using porn, they should not waste time sitting around feeling ashamed and guilty for succumbing to natural urges, but should instead regulate their use until they are able to quit permanently. Excessive guilt and shame are counterproductive and self-defeating on the Spiritual path.

Through Yoga and meditation, we discover that the sexual experience is far more than merely sexual. There is a definite connection between sexual energy and Kundalini. In the last ten years, I have experienced an interesting phenomenon several times following intense Spiritual practices such as prolonged chanting or pranayama. Generally, when this phenomenon occurs I will be lying in bed in a state of reverie somewhere in between a waking and sleeping state. Suddenly, I am thrust upright into a seated position not of my own volition and all of the vertebrae in my spine become perfectly aligned like a forceful chiropractic adjustment as a strong current of Kundalini energy surges up my spine. All of my attention is then forcibly drawn into my third eye or ajna chakra. I stare internally into the deep void of Infinity and Infinity rushes back upon itself into my Spiritual eye, and as that is occurring I have a full body orgasm. However, this orgasm involves no erection or ejaculation. There is absolutely nothing sexual about it; it is purely energetic. The entire experience lasts about two minutes or so and then I lie back down in bed and fall asleep within a few minutes. While Kundalini experiences such as these are pleasantly entertaining, they are not necessarily transformative. Many people make the mistake of confusing energetic happenings with Enlightenment. They are beneficial, but do not leave us any more Enlightened than we were before we had the experience.

The sexual experience can become more and more Spiritualized with one's partner as they both raise their levels of consciousness through a diligent Yoga and meditation practice. Tantra Yoga involves the bringing together or unification of male and female energies known as Shiva and Shakti within one's Being. Sex is an outer symbol of what is happening within during the Tantric awakening process. With practice, the sex act becomes more and more Spiritualized and is a Yoga technique in and of itself.

Sex is just a part of life, and without it souls could not incarnate here on Earth. Human beings are a frail life form and the survival rate for newborns in our storied past was low, along with life expectancy. Therefore, the sexual urge is extremely high in humans so that procreation is ensured. The instinctual drive to procreate is abnormally high in humans and chimpanzees when compared to other mammals. This is because human life is fragile in a state of nature, and in order to ensure the survival of the species, humans needed to engage in the sexual act as often as possible so that a woman could produce as many offspring as possible in her short lifetime. Of course, with modern medicine and technology, this need for constant procreation is no longer necessary and our intense sexual craving is a vestigial instinct. In fact, the most daunting problem we face as a human race is the extreme overpopulation of planet Earth. We would be wise to curtail our sexual cravings and utilize modern birth control methods in an effort to preserve dwindling natural ces for the future generations of souls incarnating here on

For any addiction, it is recommended that one regulate their habit until they can quit for good. Only a small minority of people are able to quit a habit or addiction cold turkey. For the vast majority, regulation and tapering off is the recommended method. For instance, if someone is addicted to cigarettes, then they should set a schedule for tapering off until they are able to quit completely, rather than trying to quit all at once. There is a far greater likelihood of relapse after quitting something cold turkey than there is for quitting slowly over time in a controlled manner.

When we are attempting to quit a bad habit such as smoking, drinking, or overeating, it is of vital importance to stay away from people and situations that trigger our cravings. Paramahansa Yogananda used to tell his followers that company and environment were far more important than will power when confronting a bad habit or non-useful action. If a yogi is serious about Spiritual evolution, then spending time around people who are consistently drinking, smoking, eating meat, and using drugs is detrimental. We must leave these people behind no matter how painful it might be in the beginning. We will attract people into our lives who are not interested in self-serving acts, and we will have new friends with a more positive lifestyle to spend time with. That is how it works.

Our environment and the company we keep have a profound impact on our states of mind and consciousness and we must never underestimate the importance of avoiding situations and people that no longer serve us on our Spiritual growth path. After some time, we can learn to be in any situation surrounded by any group of people and remain undisturbed, but in the beginning it is necessary to be incredibly mindful of our environment. Although, it is interesting that as we grow Spiritually we intentionally avoid environments and people that lower our vibration and consciousness, and once we are Enlightened we continue to avoid these same environments and people, not because we have to, but because we have no longer have any interest in them. Spiritually immature people tend to assume that they should be able to be in any situation unaffected and untempted because avoiding situations is a type of aversion. Avoidance of situations that tempt us to act inappropriately is not aversion; it is wisdom. We need not skip steps in the Enlightenment process and egotistically assume that we are ready to deal with any situation unaffected before our consciousness is sufficiently prepared.

In the philosophy of Yoga, there is no concept of sin. There are simply useful acts and non-useful acts on the path to Enlightenment. As conscious beings with freewill, we can either choose actions that are life enhancing or actions that are life-negating. The word sin is used in the Judeo-Christian lexicon to imply an act that will be punished by an angry God. Likewise, a virtuous act is one that will be rewarded. God is not a father figure that lives in the sky and rewards and punishes us for our actions. When we think in terms of reward and punishment, we are taking things personally. When we take things personally, we are identified with the person being rewarded or punished, which is antithetical to the Enlightenment path. Instead, we should objectively view the effects that come about as a result of our actions as having been caused by those actions. Rather than thinking in terms of reward and punishment, we should think in terms of cause and effect. The universe obeys laws of cause and effect. Judging effects as rewards and punishments is illusory. What one person considers a reward, another may consider a punishment and vice versa. There is no objective reality to this kind of childish morality; there is only the law of cause and effect. When we commit an act, it causes a corresponding effect.

The reason that we are attracted to sense pleasures is because we mistakenly believe that they will bring us happiness. Happiness, as we come to find out on the path, is highly over-rated. Happiness, or temporary satisfaction, is quickly followed by craving and suffering. Pleasure is just pain in disguise. The up and down roller coaster of pleasure and pain causes vrittis in our Being that leave us restless and unable to experience lasting peace and true contentment. It is due to our Spiritual immaturity and ignorance that we seek the quick fix and the easy way out. Most people are not even aware that there is an alternative to the roller coaster ride. Most people do not believe that it is possible to experience a permanent and lasting peace or they are too lazy to pursue it, so they continue to participate in the cycle of suffering. Many Enlightened sages throughout the ages have left us with a way to experience a lasting peace so that we can get off of the roller coaster and rest eternally in our true nature, but we need to be Spiritually mature enough to engage in the daily, disciplined practices necessary to attain this peace.

Roy Eugene Davis states the following with regards to the majority of people alive today:

> The majority of people on the planet today are impelled by their emotions, more interested in self-serving actions and relationships than in Self-discovery, and passively complacent about their present psychological and spiritual states. Their knowledge of higher realities is minimal and their hope of living beyond this incarnation, if they have such hope, is nurtured by blind faith. Although they know that physiological demise is inevitable, they avoid confronting it and do little to assure their spiritual growth and future well being.

Indulgence in sense pleasures is an inherently self-serving act (I use a lowercase s here to signify the false self). If we are in service to self, then we are sorely mistaken if we believe that we can somehow continue to indulge in sense pleasures and maintain our Spiritual practices simultaneously. Every time we indulge in sense pleasures, we are feeding, strengthening, and empowering the false self. Sense pleasure is the food of the ego, which has an insatiable appetite. The more we feed it, the hungrier it gets. Every time we drink a beer, or smoke a joint, or cheat on our spouse, we feed and empower the ego or false self. As yogis, our duty is to starve the false self, not feed it like ordinary humans. In reality, yogis are not ordinary humans. Yogis have the ability to control their reactions and states of mind and consciousness. Therefore, we must starve the hungry beast that is the ravenous ego and control our passions and cravings until they no longer remain.

The desire for sense pleasure exists because we possess samskaras, or karmic seeds. These karmic seeds leave their imprint on the mind and subtle body every time we like or dislike something. In other words, every time we experience pleasure or pain a karmic seed is planted in our false self. These seeds can only take root in the field of awareness that is identified with the temporary self/ego. Each time that we succumb to pleasure or avoid pain, we feed and nourish the seeds. We can only experience pleasure and pain from the vantage point of the false self or ego. At our core, the Infinite Consciousness does not experience pleasure or pain and once we have transcended our mistaken sense of self identity, we no are no longer subject to pleasure and pain, and we can experience Spiritual freedom. Through a disciplined practice of daily superconscious meditation, we can uproot all of our samskaras and burn them in the flames of our meditation. Samskaras must take root and grow in the ego-field and once the ego-field no longer predominates, samskaras have nowhere to grow and they are permanently extinguished.

We must have faith that there is a bliss and pleasure that is far more subtle and worthy of our attention and adoration than mere sense pleasure. There exists a secret nectar or ambrosia that enlivens and intoxicates every cell of the body in an advanced yogi. This nectar goes by many names, but it starts off as a substance referred to as soma when it is created in the brain during deep states of superconscious meditation. The yogi can taste it in the palate of the mouth as it drips down in the form of a special type of saliva from the brain. Over time, this soma makes its way down into the rest of the body and is then referred to as amrita, or Divine nectar. This is the true food of the gods spoken of in the ancient texts such as the Vedas. After enough practice and experience with superconsciousness and Samadhi, the yogi can begin to feel this ambrosia nearly all the time even when they are not formally meditating. If one is Spiritually mature and patient enough to engage in a disciplined, daily superconscious meditation practice, they can experience this Spiritual intoxication. However, it must be said that this ambrosia is not the goal of Spiritual practice. A state of Oneness that transcends all sensation ought to be our ultimate aim.

The experience of amrita is the Spiritual gift that we are given once we begin removing all that separates us from the Infinite. When we continually insult the Divine by our reliance on temporary sense pleasures for peace and happiness, we cannot experience the gift of amrita. However, if we demonstrate the patience and maturity necessary to live the life of a true yogi, we can experience a bliss and peace far greater than any sense pleasure could ever provide.

3 THE GURU

"An enlightened guru never manipulates or abuses disciples or selfishly attempts to control their thoughts or actions. Disciples are encouraged to use their own powers of discriminative intelligence, intuition, and common sense, and to wisely exercise freedom of choice."
-Roy Eugene Davis

One's relationship with the Guru is another telltale sign of their level of Spiritual maturity. From the outset, I am working from the premise that a yogi should have a Guru if they are serious about progressing on the Spiritual path. Yoga has always been taught, and more importantly transmitted, from Guru to disciple, usually one on one or in very small groups. The vast majority of the people I know who consider themselves to be yogis do not have a Guru. Treading the Spiritual path without a Guru is like trying to make it through college without professors. I am sure it might be possible, but why would anyone want to attempt it if there are well qualified, knowledgeable professors available? Most people arrogantly assume in a very immature fashion that they do not need a Guru to assist them on their Enlightenment path and that they can learn everything they need to know just by living their life and reading a few books. One need only read any ancient Yogic text (the Bhagavad Gita for instance) to realize how much importance the founders of Yoga placed on the Guru.

Until I met my Guru, Roy Eugene Davis, I was swimming in the kiddy pool of Spiritual kindergarten. After a few years spent with Mr. Davis, I went from playing around in the kiddy pool to diving into the deep end of adult Spirituality very quickly. I feel incredibly blessed to have found a real Guru who is a living embodiment of Enlightenment. Most seekers are not that fortunate and may spend many years searching hopelessly for a teacher who can properly guide them. Even if one is not fortunate enough to encounter a living Master, they ought to at the very least seek out an experienced meditation teacher who can guide them in the process and answer their questions.

When I was in my late twenties I was perusing books in the local metaphysical bookstore in Dahlonega, GA where I was living at the time. I saw <u>Autobiography of a Yogi</u> and was immediately drawn to Paramahansa Yogananda's eyes on the cover as they called out to me. I bought the book and read it in three days. I knew immediately that I had found my Spiritual path and I prayed to the Lord that I might be sent a real Guru who could guide me in the same way that Yogananda's Guru had guided him. Within a week's time, I was flipping through a metaphysical magazine when I saw an advertisement for a meditation retreat in the North Georgia Mountains near where I lived being offered by a direct disciple of Paramahansa Yogananda named Roy Eugene Davis. I knew that this was no coincidence and that my prayers had been answered. My wife and I attended the retreat and my life was forever changed.

The first time I entered the meditation hall at Center for Spiritual Awareness, everything there including the smells and sounds was completely familiar. It is difficult to put into words, but there was nothing foreign about being there; I felt right at home. Also, when I was initiated into Kriya Yoga and I learned the Kriya techniques, I remembered them all and it was not the first time I had learned them; just the first time in this incarnation. Upon the first meeting with my Guru, I had the sudden insight that it is one thing to read about Enlightened people in a book, and it is another thing altogether to experience the illuminating presence of a true Spiritual Master in person. Mr. Davis exudes an energy called Shakti-pat that is palpable and fills the space around him with Omnipresence. I was overwhelmed with feelings of omnipresence, omnipotence, and omniscience upon meeting my Guru for the first time. After my first meditation in his presence, there was no doubt that he was my Guru and that our reunion had been Divinely arranged and ordained.

Mr. Davis has the following to say concerning the Guru:

> Some people, inclined to protect their self-centered attitudes and with behaviors influenced by habits and moods, err in thinking that spiritual growth processes have changed through the centuries or that cultural circumstances determine them. One common misguided notion is that in our modern era the average person's sense of individuality and assertive inclination to demonstrate self-determined independence requires a different relationship with a truth teacher: one that might make possible the acquisition of higher knowledge and rapid spiritual growth while allowing for the preservation of the self-centered condition. Insightful analysis of the irrational idea will reveal that ego-fixated self-consciousness and illumination of consciousness cannot coexist.

The universal laws governing the process of Enlightenment do not change over time. Cultural norms and mores do not alter the basic principles of the path to Spiritual awakening. The role of the Guru is just as important now in our modern day culture as it was five thousand years ago in Ancient India. Enlightened or semi-enlightened yogis have always worked with very small groups of disciples in caves and ashrams quietly transmitting their awakened consciousness on to the next generation of teachers. It is this direct transmission from teacher to student that has maintained an unbroken line of awakened consciousness for millennia. There is no need to attempt to fix something that has never been broken just because our modern day culture values arrogant independence in place of egoless devotion to a wise teacher.

It is important to note that in traditional Yoga, a Guru historically always worked with small groups of disciples. Any modern Guru who has thousands or even millions of followers is not teaching Yoga, but instead is the leader of a personality cult or religion. Yoga cannot be transmitted and learned without the availability of a highly accessible Guru. A teacher who must constantly cope with the demands of thousands of followers will not be accessible to answer questions and transmit their consciousness to a Spiritually hungry devotee. In the Tibetan texts there are lists of the qualities that a real Guru must possess, and very high on the list is accessibility. These same texts also mention that a Guru should have few students and should have no desire for name or fame. In our modern world we must make exceptions due to the demands of so many millions of Spiritual seekers. Because of the issue of an ever increasing demand for Gurus and an incredibly small supply of legitimate Masters available to teach, Paramahansa Yogananda divided his teaching into two categories; quantity and quality.

Yogananda spoke at large gatherings all over the United States to sold out crowds of Spiritual seekers and had many members in his organization that followed his teachings. This was his quantity work. He found it necessary to plant seeds in the minds of people wherever he went, but he also wisely realized that it might be many incarnations before those seeds began to sprout. His quality teachings were for a select few who were ready to awaken in their current incarnation. He spent much more private time guiding and preparing this small group of devotees and taught them in a manner more in line with traditional Yoga. My Guru teaches in a similar manner. He has initiated more than ten thousand people in Kriya Yoga, but works quietly behind the scenes with a small group of devoted followers in a more intimate way. This ought to be the model for any modern Yoga Guru, but all too often the modern Guru is more interested in fame and wealth, and is primarily concerned with attracting a large number of followers.

There are so many examples of the moral and financial corruption of modern Yoga Gurus and sexual scandals involving the manipulation of young female devotees that I dare not venture down that path. It is truly beyond the scope of this book to go into details about the various and sundry exploits of many famous modern Gurus in the Yoga tradition, but needless to say, there are countless examples. Because of the abundance of scandals, many people assume that all Gurus are self serving, manipulative charlatans. However, just because someone discovers a few bad apples in the basket does not mean that they should throw out all the apples.

Most Gurus are not perfect and are only working from a semi-enlightened state, which means they still have some karma to work out. Because there are so few fully Liberated beings currently alive on planet Earth, most of us are left with Gurus who are still working out remaining karma. As long as we know that from the outset, there is really no problem. The problem lies in the common error that we make when we immaturely assume that a Guru must be perfect and flawless. We must realize that there are many subtle stages of Enlightenment and each Guru is working from a different stage within that wide spectrum.

Gurus are not perfect and they are not be worshipped. To worship something is to admit separation from the object of worship. For worship to occur, the subject must worship the object, which is evidence of duality. Yoga is the realization of the union of subject and object, and the realization that duality is a grand illusion, and therefore, worship has no place in the Yoga tradition. One should naturally have a good rapport with their teacher and be devoted to following their teachings, but Guru worship is generally reserved for immature, emotionally dependent people who treat the Guru as a surrogate mother or father figure. Mr. Davis has the following to say about Guru worship:

> Not all Spiritual Masters and saints who have appeared on the world scene through the centuries have been acknowledged or understood, and some have been deified and worshipped by intellectually deficient, emotionally dependent devotees who chose to admire rather than become like them.

I have met many people who love to talk incessantly about how Enlightened their Guru is. I have never understood this type of pride and adoration. What does the Guru's Enlightenment have to do with the devotee's Enlightenment? We are ultimately responsible for our own Enlightenment. It is highly beneficial to have a teacher that is authentic and knowledgeable, but the teacher's Enlightenment is their own, and is not a reflection of our state of consciousness. I know devotees who spend more time talking about how Enlightened their Guru is than they do in meditation trying to become like their Guru.

Guru worship has caused the emergence of many personality cults. There is a countless number of personality cults in India and elsewhere based upon the worship of a particular teacher. Even many of the world's most popular religions like Christianity are, in essence, personality cults. The worship of a person does not change the worshipper's inner condition or state of consciousness. This is why the path of Bhakti Yoga can only take one so far on the path to Enlightenment.

Bhakti Yoga, as it is practiced in India, generally involves the ritual worship of a particular deity or a Guru. While one may experience an emotional high from the practices of Bhakti Yoga, this high wears off and the Bhakti yogi is left no closer to Enlightenment than they were before they started. Bhakti Yoga ought to be practiced alongside meditation, but sadly, it usually is not. Most people are content to get an emotional buzz without any desire for higher understanding or Enlightenment and die never having experienced Yoga or Divine Union.

There are many personality cults based upon the worship of deceased Gurus. Christianity is one example, but there are hundreds of similar cults the world over. In order to derive benefit from the teachings of a Guru, he or she must be embodied. We cannot ask questions to a dead person. Also, many of the teachings attributed to certain teachers are unreliable and it is impossible to know what a person may or may not have said, but when we learn from an embodied teacher we can know for sure what their exact teachings are and we can engage in meaningful dialogue with them. Also, there is a direct transmission of energy and consciousness that occurs between teacher and student that cannot occur unless both teacher and student are alive. The physical presence of the teacher is not always necessary, especially now with email and the like, but if it is possible, then spending time in the presence of the teacher is preferable. However, many yogis make the mistake of becoming addicted and attached to being in the physical presence of the Guru all the time; this is no better than any other type of addiction and can be a major obstacle on the Spiritual growth path.

It is important to use discernment when choosing a Guru. There are many charlatans and posers in the world of modern Yoga and Spirituality. Mr. Davis explains it as follows:

> Involvements with charismatic or persuasive individuals who make extravagant claims about their spiritual attainment, abilities, or teachings, whose personal delusions are obvious, or whose self-interest is the primary motivation for attracting

a following, should be avoided. Although gurus provide practical advice and endeavor to attune themselves to the mind and consciousness of receptive disciples for the purpose of transmitting their inner realization, they should not be thought of as magicians to whom one might go, or pray to, with expectations of having personal problems instantly solved or miracles performed on their behalf.

Many well meaning yogis fall into the trappings of charismatic Gurus who have large followings because they long for a sense of belonging and find it in a community of devotees. With emotional and Spiritual maturity, we realize that community and a sense of belonging are really not all that important and are actually a hindrance in our Spiritual growth path. Reliance on others is a symptom of emotional dependency and should be transcended. According to my Guru, the Spiritual path is a path of aloneness. The devotee cannot take their Spiritual community with them. When we die, we die alone and return to the Infinite only to be reborn surrounded by other people in other circumstances if we are reborn on Earth. Our community changes with each passing incarnation, and we would be wise not to allow ourselves to become overly attached.

Another clever trick employed by many false Gurus is to claim that they are the reincarnation of a famous saint or Guru with no proof. This is an easy thing to do, because it is nearly impossible to prove and there are enough doughy eyed, naive people that are ready to buy into it. In the Tibetan tradition, there are many rigorous tests that must be done to ensure that a Lama or Rinpoche has reincarnated. There are some legitimate means of proving reincarnation, such as the recognition of family members from a past life or the familiarity of certain objects and even facial features and birthmarks carried over from a previous incarnation. However, in the wider world, these fail safes do not exist so anyone can claim to be the reincarnation of anyone they choose without having to prove it.

Paramahansa Yogananda once told my Guru that in the future there would be many people seeking Enlightenment and that there would not be enough qualified teachers to serve them. We have reached such a time. Finding a truly qualified Guru is becoming more and more difficult, and there are not nearly enough to serve the ever expanding population of truth seekers. The Bhagavad Gita states that only one in every thousand people possesses the capacity for Enlightenment and out of every one thousand of these individuals, only one becomes fully Enlightened. Therefore, one out of every one million people on the planet are potentially experiencing a very advanced stage of Enlightenment according to the Gita. If we extrapolate these numbers then we come to the conclusion that there are possibly seven thousand or so people experiencing very advanced stages of Enlightened consciousness on Earth right now given that the Earth's current population is around seven billion (and not all Enlightened people choose to teach). Obviously, for the many millions of truth seekers and yogis on the Enlightenment path, there are not enough Enlightened Gurus to go around. However, when a seeker is adequately prepared, a Guru will appear in their life; it has always been so.

One need not spend years searching for the Guru. Once a student is ready, a Guru appears. If a yogi spends years searching unsuccessfully for a Guru, it is because their consciousness is not yet prepared to grasp the teachings that an Enlightened person has to offer them. Likewise, there are those people who hear about a friend's Guru and perhaps attend a few lectures or satsangs and derive no benefit. They may even engage in a conversation or two with the Guru only to realize quickly that they do not resonate with the Guru or his or her teachings. They then assume that the reason they do not resonate with the Guru is because they require a different Guru, rather than coming to the more logical conclusion that they simply have not reached a point in their Spiritual evolution where they are ready to handle a mature Guru-disciple relationship. When the student is ready, the Guru appears; this universal law of cause and effect has not changed over the millennia.

Mr. Davis shares his thoughts on the matter as follows:

> Those who desire a casual relationship with a Guru or enlightenment tradition, are like voyeurs who enjoy observing the object of their interest from a hidden vantage point or dilettantes whose participation is superficial and amateurish. They are not sincerely interested in learning how to grow spiritually. If allowed personal access to a teacher, they waste the teacher's time and energies as well as their own.

I have observed this time and again with the meditation retreat participants at Center for Spiritual Awareness, many of whom maintain only a casual, immature relationship with Mr. Davis. He told me recently that out of the over ten thousand people who he has initiated, only about ten percent maintained any kind of long term relationship with him and only a percentage of those followers were fully committed to their practices and Spiritual Enlightenment. Most people are so deeply entrenched in identification with their personality-selves that they do not possess the capacity to fully put into practice what the Guru has to offer by way of his or her teachings.

Many seekers are attracted to Gurus who inflate, nurture, and coddle their egos. Many Spiritually immature people flock to Gurus who tell them that because they have found him or her, they are very Spiritually advanced. Many fake Gurus, in an attempt to attract and keep followers, fill their devotees ever-growing heads with compliments and assurances that they are highly advanced beings due to their relationship with him or her. The Gurus even give their devotees special Sanskrit names or create "inner circles" where only the highest and most advanced disciples can belong. With a little investigation, it becomes quite clear that these inner circles are almost always populated by the followers with the most money or the highest capacity to attract more followers into the fold. Many Gurus are masters not of Spirituality, but of manipulation to an almost Machiavellian degree. It is not the job of the Guru to nurture one's ego or personality-self; quite the contrary. It is the Guru's sacred duty to sever one's identification with the ego. Sometimes this requires the Guru to be quite harsh or brusque at times, but we find that tough love is usually what is takes to destroy the ego's stranglehold over us.

My Guru has never asked anyone for money and his small organization has always operated on voluntary donations from people who attend meditation retreats and his devotees. Seekers must always be wary of any Guru or organization charging exorbitant fees for retreats, workshops, lectures, and seminars, especially when there is excessive pressure to attend the events for fear of being "left out" or ostracized. The Guru-disciple relationship is not a for-profit business. It is a Spiritual exchange based on mutual respect and unconditional love. Once money becomes involved, it often taints the purity and sanctity of the relationship and the free exchange of energy and consciousness.

Large Spiritual organizations that require huge sums of money to operate should be avoided. Small organizations that promote the teacher and his or her teachings at a low cost are preferable. In the past, there were no organizations for Yoga Gurus, but in our modern era with the booming population and mass media, it has become a near necessity. However, as yogis, we should guard against the uncontrolled growth of organizations whose primary interest is growth. Again, when the organizations become too large, they begin to form new religious movements and personality cults that negate the very purpose of the Guru-disciple relationship. Yoga teachings must be transmitted from Guru to disciple through the act of initiation, and then ordination for those students who become teachers themselves. This is the way it has always been, and the advent of new technologies and/or cultural norms and mores changes nothing.

Initiation is an indispensable facet of the Guru-disciple relationship. It is through Yoga initiation that we receive the blessings of the Guru and the transmission of consciousness that occurs between Guru and disciple. Many so called yogis are not even aware that initiation is an integral part of the Yoga tradition. They mistakenly assume that they can garner information from books and videos and do not need to be personally initiated by a Guru. Information in books is useful of course, but there is no energetic transmission that occurs when something is learned from a book or video. Authentic Yoga has always been an initiatory practice. In fact, if one considers themselves to be a yogi, but has never participated in an initiation ceremony with a bona fide Yoga Guru of a legitimate lineage of Enlightened Masters, it is like someone who considers themselves to be a doctor having never graduated from medical school.

There is a direct transmission of Spiritual force and consciousness that exists amongst the lineage of Gurus in a legitimate Yoga tradition. I am a teacher in the Kriya Yoga tradition and every time I do an initiation service, I feel the surge of this Divine transmission flowing through me like a raging river. This only occurs in authentic Yoga traditions where the transmission of awakened consciousness is passed from teacher to student, generation to generation. The more Enlightened the Masters of a tradition are, the more powerful the transmission of consciousness that occurs from Guru to disciple. It is important to note that this transmission can only occur when and if the student is receptive. If a student is not receptive due to an insufficiently prepared nervous system or perhaps due to his or her clinging to provincial beliefs, then the transmission cannot flow smoothly. This is akin to having static in a radio signal. We must fully prepare ourselves to receive what a Guru has to offer, otherwise our Spiritual antenna will not be able to "tune in" to the transmission that the Guru is transmitting.

Everything in the manifest multiverse is vibratory. All matter emits a frequency, and to go a step further, all matter comes from frequency. In reality, there are two ways in which we can discuss the manifest realm, in terms of particles, or in terms of vibratory waves, but for the purposes of describing metaphysical themes, we typically use waves, and not particles. Even the vacuum of space, that we would typically think of as empty, is oscillating at an incredibly high frequency. In fact, within this vacuum, there is enough potential energy within one cubic centimeter to power all the electricity on the entire planet. All is vibratory with the exception of Pure Consciousness, which does not vibrate; it is complete stillness. There have been many recent experiments demonstrating through Cymatics how sound frequencies coalesce into specific forms based upon the media used, and the Hz and volume of the sound. Being in the physical presence of a true Master is a veritable symphony of Divine transmissions that have a physical and energetic effect on our Being, raising our vibration and vitalizing our consciousness. However, we must be doing the Spiritual work so that every layer of our Being is able to receive the frequencies that are being transmitted by the Guru. There is a particular technique within the Kriya tradition known as Omkar Kriya that is especially useful for attuning our Being to the Divine frequencies that a Master resonates. If the reader is not yet a Kriya initiate, I highly recommend seeking out a qualified Kriya teacher to learn the ancient and powerful techniques of Kriya Yoga.

I hear from many people on the Spiritual path that they do not require a Guru because the "inner Guru" is the real Guru and they can learn everything they need to know from within. While this is ultimately true, the people that claim this are not ready to hear what the inner Guru has to tell them because they have not done the preparatory work first with an outer Guru. In fact, most of the people that have told me this do not even meditate or do any Spiritual work at all. It is simply another excuse that they use not to engage in a mature relationship with a Guru or pursue a Spiritual growth path. It is the absolute highest truth that we have within us all knowledge of the universe and its processes and that we require nothing from the outside to awaken to Self-Realization. However, in a more practical, realistic sense, an outer Guru can lead us to the inner Guru. At some point in our Spiritual journey the outer Guru may become obsolete once we have learned all that we need to learn from him or her. However, this is a more advanced stage of the awakening process and is not the first step like some inexperienced, naive seekers seem to think.

I find it interesting that in the West we are so quick to solicit the expertise of a teacher for almost every aspect of our lives whether it be a fitness instructor, college professor, private tutor, driving instructor, career coach, or any other type of expert in a field, and yet we are hesitant to seek out a Spiritual teacher to help us understand and unlock the secrets of consciousness and the universe. If our primary aim in life is not to understand our relationship with the Infinite and to uncover the secret workings of the cosmos, then our life is wasted. We are given an incredible opportunity on this planet in these bodies to explore and discover the great mystery of life and awaken to our fullest potential and yet, the majority of us are more concerned with the comings and goings of celebrities and the outcomes of sporting events.

"God, transcending time, space, and karma, is the true Guru, the teacher of even the ancient teachers."
-Patanjali

4 DISCIPLINE

"The practitioner of yoga should steadily contemplate the supreme Reality, in solitude, alone, with the mind and body controlled, having no cravings for anything. In a clean, suitable place, established in a firm meditation posture, there, intent upon practice, with thoughts and senses subdued, let the devotee practice meditation to purify the mind. With body and head erect, motionless, gazing into the spiritual eye with focused attention, serene, fearless, established in a vow of self-control, concentrating on that Supreme Reality, one should steadfastly sit, devoted to the highest realization."
-The Bhagavad Gita 6:10-14

Discipline is an integral component of a Spiritually mature life. Without discipline, the ultimate goals of Self-Realization, God-Realization, and complete Liberation of consciousness are nearly impossible. One cannot hope to attain any degree of Enlightened consciousness without a disciplined practice of daily meditation. Discipline is the key with which we may unlock the doors of the Infinite. There are those who would point out that a few individuals have simply woken up without a daily meditation practice. While this is true, it is incredibly rare and is certainly the exception rather than the rule. A sure sign of Spiritual immaturity is the avoidance of meditation due to the fact that handful of people in the history of mankind have awakened without it. The ego/mind will create almost any excuse not to engage in a disciplined meditation practice.

The false self abhors meditation. It views meditation as its certain demise and lives in total fear of losing its stranglehold over our Being. Therefore, the false self will stop at nothing to prevent us from maintaining a disciplined meditation practice. It will create excuses why we should not meditate, it will manifest annoying thoughts, memories, and fears, and it will do anything within its power to maintain its control. There is a universal law in the universe; those in power wish to remain in power. We can see this demonstrated in dictatorial regimes currently reigning over countries like North Korea and Zimbabwe. This is why modern democratic nations have wisely implemented term limits as a safeguard to prevent tyranny. Likewise, the universe wisely implemented term limits for us as well known as incarnations. The false identity is never allowed to dominate us completely since it dies at the end of each life-cycle. However, we do allow it to dominate us completely during each life until we are fully Self-Realized.

The ego/false-self maintains its dominance over our Being as a survival mechanism meant to keep us alive. It has served us well in its Darwinian purpose during our physical evolution here on planet Earth. Through a process of natural selection and survival of the fittest, our ego has become more and more solidified and realistic. That is why consciousness has become so fixated and identified with the ego over the millennia. The more realistic the matrix-illusion becomes, the more consciousness becomes seduced by it. However, we are reaching a point in our collective evolution like never before where we are able to step outside the illusion and observe it from a detached perspective. This is primarily due to the fact that we no longer need to be as wholly identified with ego to assure our survival as we did in the past.

Much of our need for the identification with ego centers around survival. This manifests in various ways, but much of it has to do with our survival in tribal groupings; humans are, after all, pack animals. The ego is always defending itself against attack and attempting to climb social ladders to ensure access to food and potential mates within the tribe or subgroup. However, we are reaching a point in our socio-cultural evolution where we are beginning to realize that we no longer must depend on our social standing for food. Even if no one likes or accepts me, I can still access food in our modern world (potential mates might be trickier!).

In the past, we needed to have the acceptance of our tribe in order to procure food and other necessities such as water, shelter, heat, etc...This is no longer true. Therefore, our ego no longer serves the great purpose that it once did. We are free to choose not to identify with it and it will not have the same survival consequences that it did in the past. This is an amazing time Spiritually to be alive. It is a time in which our collective consciousness may evolve to never before seen levels of Spiritual maturity. Ever since the dawn of sentience, language, and self-reflective capabilities, Enlightenment has most likely been possible for humans, but within this new cultural context, it seems we have been given a unique opportunity for Spiritual growth and evolution.

However, even within this new cultural context, the process of Enlightenment itself has not changed. There is a step by step disciplined process that we must all go through in order to attain Self-Realization. There is an interesting misnomer that I hear often from inexperienced people within Spiritual circles, which states that there are many paths that lead to Enlightenment. This is simply false. There is only one path; the path of awakening from ego-consciousness to Infinite consciousness, or Self-Realization. This path may look slightly different for people within different cultures and religious systems on the outside, but the actual process occurring on the inside is always the same. Religious beliefs regarding God, creation, the afterlife, and the like are irrelevant and have nothing to do with the path from ego based consciousness to Oneness consciousness, or Self-Realization. There is only one step by step process that will lead us to our goal on the Enlightenment path and luckily it was written down about two thousand years ago in ancient India by a man named Patanjali.

In the Yoga Sutras of Patanjali, there is a list of eight limbs, or steps that a yogi must follow on a daily basis if they wish to attain Samadhi, and ultimately permanent Self-knowing, also known as Self-Realization. This is the original Ashtanga Yoga (eight limbed Yoga), and should not be confused with its modern derivative invented by Pattabhi Jois, which is basically just asana and only represents one of the eight limbs described by Patanjali.

The eight limbs are as follows: 1. yamas and 2. niyamas (moral/ethical code), 3. asana (comfortable, upright seated position), 4. pranayama (breathing techniques meant to liberate the movement of prana in the system and guide it upward toward the higher chakras), 5. pratyahara (retirement of the senses), 6. dharana (concentration of the mind using a technique such as mantra), 7. dhyana (superconscious meditation), and 8. Samadhi (Oneness consciousness). When we properly practice steps three through seven in order on a daily basis, over time we can succeed in experiencing Samadhi and ultimately full Enlightenment. This is the promise of a disciplined Yoga practice. In other traditions such as Christianity, we are told that we are wretched sinners and below God. In the Yoga tradition, we are told that we have the potential to experience what Christ experienced and become Christ-like, and that we are always at one with God.

There are many seekers who try the procedures ascribed by Patanjali for a year or two without success and give up on their quest not realizing that we are meant to engage in these practices every day for the rest of our lives without fail until we reach our goal. Patanjali states in the Yoga Sutras that success in Yoga requires a long time. If we think about our sojourn in terms of many multiple incarnations, then a year or two is really nothing. We have most likely spent many incarnations accumulating karma and a false identification with matter so we cannot expect to shatter our illusion in a matter of a few years. I personally know many sincere yogis who have been practicing for decades and still have not had nearly as much success as they would like.

Swami Rama, a famous and prominent yogi who spent many years studying with real Himalayan Yoga Masters in caves, claimed in his autobiography that it took him seventeen years before he had his first Samadhi experience. I was fortunate and blessed enough to experience Oneness after about four years of ardent practice, but needless to say, it requires a great deal of time, effort, and most importantly, discipline. There is no hard and fast rule for how long one must practice before their first Samadhi experience, but generally it requires years if not decades. However, we ought to have the expectation that we can and will experience Samadhi every time we sit to meditate or even while we are engaged in our mundane daily activities. Paramahansa Yogananda used to say that we should seek God with Infinite intensity every day, but that we should also have Infinite patience just in case we do not find God that day. He also said that we should meditate more deeply each day than we did the day before. This is not always possible, but it is certainly an inspiring ambition.

We must also understand that Samadhi is not really the ultimate goal of Yoga. Samadhi is a temporary experience; a temporary glimpse at Enlightenment. Many people may experience a brief glimpse, but remain largely unchanged and return to ordinary states of consciousness after the experience has subsided. However, there is a form of Self-knowing referred to as Kaivalya, which is a permanent state. There are many words associated with this state of being such as Self-Realization or full Enlightenment, but essentially it is a permanent state of complete Self-knowing. Once in this permanent state, we never return to our former limited states. There is a state of being even beyond Self-Realization known as Liberation or Moksha. We can be Self-Realized, but still working out previous karma accumulated before we became Self-Realized. However, once Self-Realized, it is impossible for us to accumulate new karma because the karma has no false self to attach itself to; it has nowhere to land. There are many examples of Self-Realized Masters who continue to behave in ways unbecoming of a true Master and this is because they are not yet fully Liberated. At any given time on planet Earth, there are very few fully Liberated Masters. I will not speculate as to an approximate number, but the reason there are so few is because it is incredibly difficult to accomplish complete Liberation, and once Liberated, a Master typically does not return to planet Earth, but remains in refined astral or causal realms to continue his or her evolution there.

Without some degree of Spiritual maturity, discipline is impossible. A real measuring stick for Spiritual maturity is one's level of discipline with regards to their Spiritual practices. For example, someone who meditates on an irregular basis cannot be considered a serious, mature yogi. For a Spiritually mature yogi, each day is treated as an opportunity for full awakening, and Enlightenment is always their top priority in life. Therefore, sadhana or Spiritual practice is likewise a yogi's top priority for each and every day that they are incarnated.

Routine is vital to maintaining tapas, or Spiritual discipline. Most Gurus recommend meditating at the same time every day. In this way, it becomes a part of our daily routine just like brushing our teeth, showering, and eating meals. When something becomes part of our normal daily schedule, we do not have to think about it and it becomes automatic. The ego will try anything within its power to prevent us from establishing meditation as part of our daily routine. It will create excuses for why we cannot and should not meditate, and it even has the power to unconsciously manifest scheduling conflicts, and in extreme cases, physical illnesses that prevent us from meditating. We must always be cognizant of the trickery of the tyrannical ego.

Meditating first thing in the morning is best. In this way, we prioritize our Spiritual awakening over everything else in our lives. By inserting meditation as the first activity in our daily schedule, we send the message to our entire Being that Spiritual awakening has become our top priority. If we wake up and check social media and email, or turn on the television to watch the news, then we are sending the message to ourselves that social concerns, or entertainment and distraction are our top priorities. It is also a good idea to schedule a second meditation either in the early evening or before bedtime. In doing so, we are allowing ourselves the opportunity to clean up any karmic debris that we may have accumulated throughout our day. Most Gurus say that meditating twice a day is far superior to meditating only once a day. I can personally attest to this. My meditations became exponentially better when I added a second meditation in the evening.

My Guru, in his writings, often recommends writing down our daily activities and creating a schedule with all the times written down for each activity, and then performing each activity at the same time every day. For some, this may seem "boring" or it may seem to lack spontaneity. However, for one on the path to Enlightenment, "fun" and "entertainment" are not prioritized as high as sadhana and Spiritual awakening. There is certainly nothing wrong with having fun, as long as it is not at the expense of maintaining our daily meditation routine. For example, if I know that I meditate everyday at 6am and 8pm, then I will not schedule other activities for those times, and I will not do anything that will disrupt that schedule like staying up late to watch a television program or going out late to see a concert or movie so that I am able to wake up early to meditate. Likewise, I will not schedule anything that might interfere with my 8pm meditation. Yogananda used to say that we should make an appointment with God everyday and make sure we keep the appointment (he was referring to meditation).

It is always interesting to see a list of our daily activities and how much time we spend doing each activity. For example, until we write it down and really think about it, we have no sense of how much time we actually spend each day on things like social media and watching television. Most Americans spend an average of three hours a day watching television and about the same amount of time on the Internet. Obviously this time would be better spent eliminating negative samskaras, rather than planting more in the subconscious via mass media and pop culture.

For the vast majority of people, restructuring their priorities is difficult. Many habits are hard to break. However, with an iron will, good company, and strong devotion, we can overcome anything. We are Unbounded Infinite Consciousness and are superior to our moods and habits. We have been given free will and can make choices using our intellect no matter how difficult that may seem at first. I have personally been able to overcome addictions, bad habits, and even heal Crohn's disease through my devotional adherence to a disciplined, daily, superconscious meditation practice.

It is important that we do our best to meditate to a state of superconsciousness every time we sit to practice. There are many meditators who are only scratching the surface when they meditate. They may elicit a tranquil, calm state that helps them relax and destress the nervous system, but this type of meditation, while beneficial, is not Spiritually transformative. It is only by meditating to a state of superconsciousness on a daily basis that we can begin to experience the true Spiritual benefits of a daily meditation practice.

Superconsciousness is a state of consciousness above or superior to the ordinary states of ego based consciousness being experienced by 99.99% of the human population. In a state of superconsciousness the mind is calm without strong or distracting thoughts, and there is a distinct sense of detachment from the mind and its contents, and we feel as though we are other than our finite ego-self. In this state, we are able to experience the sense of being an objective observer of our thoughts, rather than an active participant in them. However, this is not Samadhi. It is a preliminary state. In a superconscious state there is still an observer and that which is observed; a state of duality. In Samadhi there is no separation between observer and observed; they are one and the same.

When we meditate to a state of superconsciousness there are certain superconscious influences that have a beneficial effect on the physical, astral, and causal bodies of which our Being is composed. The physical self is rather obvious and requires no explanation, our astral self is composed of a system of chakras and nadis (energetic centers and channels) and also the lower mind (manas), and our causal self is composed primarily of the higher mind (vijnana), a sense of individuality, and also the sheath of Spiritual bliss (ananda). For a further explanation of the subtle bodies, see my book The Sacred Science of Yoga and the Five Koshas. Superconsciousness allows the nervous system to relax and detoxify and it is in the state of superconsciousness that soma and amrita are produced. Soma/amrita nourishes the brain, nervous system, and ultimately every cell of the physical body with an indescribable nectar or ambrosia. It is in superconscious states that we can begin to create a body of nectar or a yogic body that leads to exceptional physical health. A yogic body is not created by doing complicated physical postures, but rather by consistently eliciting superconscious states of being. There have been many University level studies detailing the many health benefits of meditation but they include improvements in immune system function, lymphatic function, endocrine function, digestive function, brain function, a slowing of the aging process, etc...

Spiritual growth and evolution requires work. There are many simple minded Spiritual teachers that say that all one must do to experience Enlightenment is to accept everything as it is. This implies that we should accept our current ego-based consciousness and all of our faults. I have never known or heard of anyone who has become Enlightened from making the intellectual decision to accept things as they are and nothing more. One may easily try this for themselves and observe just how quickly they immediately return to emotionally reactive states of non-acceptance. We must do the daily practices to cultivate states of acceptance and contentment. It does not happen on its own or by making an intellectual decision to be accepting. We have to do the work. My Guru, in his lectures, often talks about people who email him saying that their practices are not working. And he likes to respond to them by saying, "It's because you are not working it."

I have received hundreds of emails from people interested in learning Kriya Yoga. I email them back and ask to speak with them about learning the preliminary practices that they must do for three months before I will initiate them into the higher practices of Kriya (the preliminary practices prepare the brain and nervous system for Kriya). Upon learning that they must commit to a daily pranayama and meditation practice for three months, they discontinue their communication with me. Little do they realize that during initiation, one commits to meditating every day for the rest of their lives. Out of the many hundreds of people who have emailed me to learn Kriya, only a handful have committed to the preliminary practices for a three month period. I also offer Yoga teacher trainings through the Yoga Alliance and as part of the training I require the students to meditate daily. Out of the hundreds of people that have been certified through my program, only a few have committed to the daily practices and asked me for Kriya initiation at the end of the training. Most people simply do not want to alter their habits and routines and do the work necessary to experience Spiritual evolution. Furthermore, most people are complacently content to remain in ego based consciousness chasing sense pleasures and living in complete Spiritual ignorance.

I have heard many people (I used to be one of them) claim that meditation is not necessary and that we just need to "be present." Eckhart Tolle has popularized this idea via his popular books and many television appearances. While I enjoy his lectures and writings, I strongly disagree with his fundamental premise that all we need to do is be present without the use of techniques or practices to increase our capacity to experience pure presence. What he fails to realize is that the vast majority of people do not possess the ability to enter into presence at will and require tried and true techniques and practices to be in a state of presence. With a daily meditation practice, we can learn to be present at all times, but it requires work and devotion to our path. Many lazy seekers love Eckhart Tolle's teachings because he does not recommend a daily meditation practice. There are no shortcuts to Enlightenment.

In Chile, where I live, there are many advertisements for weekend workshops involving "quick Enlightenment" or "pineal gland activation". One simply cannot become Enlightened or activate their pineal gland in one weekend. Anyone offering workshops such as these is a charlatan or completely delusional. We must always use our discernment when attending workshops, seminars, or retreats offering "shortcut" techniques. The only real "shortcut" to Enlightenment is daily superconscious meditation. However, this shortcut generally requires decades of diligent practice, and would not be considered a shortcut by most people looking to become Enlightened in a weekend workshop.

For one who does not practice daily superconscious meditation, it may require them many thousands of incarnations to work through their karma and false identity until they reach a state of Enlightened consciousness through natural evolution. When put into perspective, decades of diligent meditation practice is indeed a shortcut relative to thousands or millions of potential incarnations. In the Kriya Yoga tradition it is thought that one Kriya pranayama done properly is equal to one year of natural Spiritual evolution unaided. Therefore, one thousand Kriya pranayamas done properly is equivalent to one thousand years of normal evolution. Myself, along with thousands of other Kriya yogis, can personally attest to the accelerated rate of Spiritual unfoldment that occurs when performing advanced Yoga techniques like Kriya on a daily basis.

Looking for Spiritual shortcuts or weekend workshops that promise instantaneous Enlightenment is a sure sign of Spiritual immaturity. An unwillingness to do the work necessary to grow Spiritually is likewise a clear indication that one is not mature enough yet to engage in a serious Spiritual growth path. People who believe they can meditate on an irregular basis only when they "feel like it," seriously underestimate the power of the ego and the seduction of maya. For example, I have met many people who attend a Vipassana ten day meditation retreat and do not meditate again until they attend another retreat. Instead, they attend the retreat and then proceed to tell everyone they know that they attended the retreat, and then they do not continue to practice what they learned during the retreat. Most people that I have met only attend Vipassana retreats as a sort of rite of passage to impress their friends with. There are, of course, exceptions.

Retreats are a good idea for those on a Spiritual growth path, but if meditation is a practice, then practicing everyday is obviously far superior to practicing for ten days and then returning to a normal lifestyle and state of being. Discipline is about committing to a daily practice, rather than committing to a ten day retreat so you can brag about it afterwards. However, it is recommended to attend at least one or two retreats a year because it gives us the opportunity to completely unplug from our normal duties and responsibilities so that we can dive deep into the Infinite for a few days without distraction. If one finds his or herself having the desire to attend retreats all the time, then they are probably best suited for the life of a renunciate or monk.

In Yoga, there are two paths; renunciate and householder. Renunciates live in cloistered, monastic environments and householders maintain a normal family and work life in the world. The path one chooses depends on their specific personality and karmic makeup. Neither path is superior to the other, no matter what most renunciates claim to the contrary. Each path has its positive and negative characteristics. For example, discipline is far easier to maintain in a monastic environment because mediation practice is usually built in to the daily schedule and everyone in the environment is participating. Because of this, one might assume that Spiritual progress would occur much more quickly for renunciates, and in some ways, it does occur more quickly. However, there is much to be learned in the world through our daily interactions with family, friends, co-workers, etc... Also, the path to maturity is quickened by our decision making in the world as it concerns finances, work, education, relationships, etc... Therefore, as is often the case, a renunciate may experience some degree of awakening only to return to the world and find out very quickly that they still have a long way to go. The world tests our Enlightenment. A renunciate's Enlightenment is a frail, fragile Enlightenment, whereas a householder's Enlightenment may take longer to attain, but once attained, has been tested by the trials and tribulations of the world and is more likely to persist.

Again, neither path is superior and one is free to choose either path based upon their karma and personality characteristics. It is entirely possible to grow to emotional and Spiritual maturity in either environment. It must be said, however, that discipline is far more difficult to maintain for householders because of their extra duties and responsibilities and work schedules. Although, if a householder is truly devoted to the path, then accommodations will be made to ensure that meditation is a part of their daily routine.

The Sanskrit word for discipline, tapas, is related to heat and fire. A similar word, tapasya, refers to a personal endeavor of discipline undertaken to achieve a goal and is also associated with heat. Likewise, it is common to hear Gurus refer to the "fires of meditation" and the "burning of karma." There exists a distinct relationship between Spiritual discipline and heat. In fact, many of the rituals and ceremonies found in the Vedas deal with making sacrifices to a fire while chanting verses in Sanskrit for the purposes of ridding oneself of karma and bringing about good fortune in one's life. Therefore, much of the symbolism in Yoga is related to fire, the sun, and heat in general.

If we think of a sap filled log placed in a fire, it becomes an apt analogy for the process of eliminating karma during superconscious meditation. When a fresh log is placed in a fire, the sap trapped within it must rise to the surface before it is able to burn off and disappear. Without extreme heat, the sap remains trapped within. Likewise, without the tapas of meditation, our karma or subconscious tendencies remain trapped within our Being. It is necessary for this karma to rise to the surface in order for it to "burn" and be eliminated. Without the fires of superconscious meditation, the karma remains lodged within our Being and never rises to the surface to be neutralized and dealt with. During meditation, we may even begin to feel a type of heat within the body. This is normal and should be observed objectively without reaction until it subsides. There are even Tibetan monks who are able to keep their bodies warm sitting in sub-freezing temperatures in the snowy slopes of the Himalayas using an advanced technique known as the "inner sun." Many people avoid and fear meditation because they are afraid to face whatever might bubble up to the surface during meditation. Avoiding looking at our faults and painful memories only postpones our progress on the Spiritual path.

It is advisable to have a suitable location in one's abode in which to meditate. Environment is important when considering one's meditation space. It should be clean and free of clutter with little to no noise. We need to be free of distractions when we meditate in order to practice pratyahara, or the internalization of the senses. If one lives in a city where there is a large amount of noise, they should use earplugs or headphones to eliminate any possible distractions to concentration. The ancient yogis practiced in caves for a reason; it was not a coincidence. Caves are utterly silent and free from distractions. However, one does not need to travel to the mountains to have a cave; we can create a cave in our home right where we are. I recommend having a simple altar with a few pictures of inspirational saints or sages, and perhaps a few quartz crystals or other decorative items.

The comfort of one's meditation seat or chair is paramount. We need not sit on the floor in lotus posture to meditate successfully. In fact, for most people this is an obstacle rather than a helpful technique. There is nothing wrong with simply sitting in a chair, especially for Westerners. Patanjali describes the correct meditation posture as any upright, comfortable posture. Therefore, it is not recommended to lay down to meditate due to our body's natural inclination to fall asleep in that position. Many people naively assume that they must be able to sit for long periods of time cross legged in the floor before they can begin meditating and conveniently use their discomfort as an excuse not to meditate. Through a daily asana practice we can become somewhat more flexible and eventually it is possible for most of us to sit on the floor for extended periods, but it is far from necessary.

When we have a lovely space in which to do our Spiritual practices, discipline becomes far easier. We sincerely begin to look forward to our daily meditation as a way to be in a Spiritually charged environment that is different than our normal surroundings. We look forward to the daily opportunity to disconnect from our ego-selves and melt into the deep peace and tranquility of the Infinite. We begin having profound insights into the nature of reality and consciousness and we eagerly anticipate the new discoveries that can be had each and every time we sit.

In the Bhagavad Gita there are four types of Yoga mentioned; Karma, Bhakti, Jnana, and Raja. Karma Yoga is the Yoga of selfless action in the world. Bhakti Yoga is the Yoga of devotion and compassion. Jnana Yoga is the Yoga of deep inquiry and intellectual study. And finally, Raja Yoga is the Yoga of direct experience of the Divine through pranayama, pratyahara, dharana, dhyana (superconscious meditation), and Samadhi. While Karma, Bhakti, and Jnana Yogas are important and should be practiced by all yogis, they do not lead to Enlightenment. It is only through Raja (translated as royal or superior) that we can reach the ultimate goals of Samadhi, Self-Realization, and Liberation. Therefore, if we return for a moment to our original definition of a yogi as one who practices Yoga (Samadhi or Union), then anyone who only practices Bhakti, Karma, or Jnana Yoga without Raja, is not actually practicing Yoga and cannot be considered a serious yogi.

I have met many people in the United States who claim to be yogis because they like to chant kirtan, which is a form of Sanskrit chanting. These people do not do pranayama, asana, or meditate or any other activities that we would commonly associate with Yoga and they certainly are not attempting to become Self-Realized. They simply enjoy the emotional high they get when they chant. In fact, many of the people I know who attend kirtans like to smoke marijuana before the kirtan because this enhances the sensory stimulation and emotional high that can be experienced during kirtan. This is certainly not Yoga. It is more akin to a rock concert or something of that nature and has nothing to do with Enlightenment. I personally love attending kirtans and there is most definitely great Spiritual benefit that can derived from Sanskrit chanting. However, we must use the clear and elevated states elicited from kirtan to dive deep into the ocean of meditation and not to get high for a couple of hours, only to return to our normal ego-based consciousness shortly thereafter.

Raja Yoga or the superior path requires discipline. For those who do not possess discipline, Bhakti, Karma, and Jnana Yogas may suffice. However, for anyone serious about Enlightenment, there is only one path of Yoga that will satisfy their inner yearning for Divine Union and that is Raja. Raja is the path of the mature, disciplined yogi intent on Self-Realization. Bhakti, Karma, and Jnana Yoga become quite natural and effortless for the Raja yogi. Once yogis begins to experience higher states of consciousness through their Raja Yoga practices, the other three Yogas become automatic; this cannot be said of the other three. That is why Raja is considered the royal or superior path. It automatically takes care of the other three Yogas and is the most direct route to Enlightenment.

Furthermore, Raja Yoga/meditation is actually the highest form of Karma Yoga. As we meditate, not only are we cleansing and purifying our own consciousness, but because we are all connected, we are literally cleansing and purifying the collective consciousness of which we are all a part. My Guru often says, "When one person wakes up, it benefits everyone because the collective consciousness is made a little bit brighter." One of the best things we can do to help others is to commit to a daily superconscious meditation practice. Most people assume that performing Karma Yoga is all about volunteering in a soup kitchen or nursing home, but this is a fairly shallow appraisal of Karma Yoga. Volunteer work is wonderful, but it is just a small part of the larger reality of Karma Yoga.

When one first embarks on the path of Spiritual discipline, they may encounter obstacles and difficulties. Beginning meditators must grapple with the resistance presented by the revolting ego. The ego views meditation as an affront to its position of dominance within our Being. It will do anything and everything within its power to maintain its control. The false self will find any excuse at its disposal to quell our attempts at Spiritual freedom and Enlightenment. It is a survival mechanism and is completely natural. Anything that is in danger will rush to defend itself from attack; the ego is no different. However, we must be prepared to strike at the ego with an iron will as it launches its defensive maneuvers. Our offense is a daily meditation practice that ignores the demands of the ego.

The ego may be thought of as a small, rebellious child who throws temper tantrums to attract the attention of his or her parents. The parent who acquiesces and gives in to the whining child's demands for attention can expect many more temper tantrums in the future. However, the parent who ignores the child's demands for attention notices quickly that the tantrums cease over time. When we give attention to something, we empower it. When we ignore something, we empower our ability to sustain states of non-reactive objectivity. It is this non-reactive objectivity that is essential for success on the Enlightenment path.

The most common error that new yogis make is trying meditation for a few weeks and deciding that it is impossible to quiet the mind and concentrate. A few weeks is not nearly enough time to begin experiencing prolonged thought free states, which only occur after a year or more in most cases. I even know of people who relate to me that they have been meditating for decades and still never experience a completely thought free state. I have a great deal of respect for these people because they have not given up hope and they continue to try. However, these cases are the exception. Most yogis, after a few months or years of meditation, are able to experience deep, thought free, superconscious states. However, these beautiful, thought free states only happen with a dedicated, daily practice. We cannot expect to have success in meditation with only an irregular practice.

Another common obstacle that beginning meditators face is the mind's tendency to make to-do lists during their attempts to meditate. If one is experiencing this phenomenon, I suggest making a to-do list at night before going to sleep, and possibly even writing down a schedule of the following day's activities. In doing so, we can start each day with a clean slate and focus on the matter at hand (meditation), rather than focusing on what we have to do that day.

I hear from many parents that they simply do not have time to meditate because they have children. This should not be an impediment to our practice. In fact, parents are usually the most stressed out group of people that I encounter in my Yoga and meditation classes and they could truly benefit from the calming effects of mediation. I usually advise that parents take turns watching the kids while the other meditates and then switch, allowing sufficient time for both partners to meditate. In the case of single parent households, the subject of meditation becomes ever more complicated. Single parents are at a slight disadvantage on the Spiritual awakening path and my heart goes out to them, but it is not impossible to find time to meditate. It is never impossible. Yogananda used to say that we should never allow the word impossible to enter our minds. If we are sincerely devoted to the Enlightenment path, the universe has a way of organizing itself around us and providing us with exactly what we need when we need it in our pursuit of the Divine. With faith, we can accomplish any goal we focus our attention on with clear intent and purpose. Attention is not enough, and intention is not enough. We must use both attention and intention to attract positive circumstances and events into our lives.

Discipline and Spiritual maturity requires that we reorganize our lives and priorities around our daily Spiritual practice and that we maintain self control in our day to day activities. For many beginning yogis, this radical change in lifestyle can come as quite a shock. It is very easy for us to slip back into old habits and patterns quickly if we are not constantly vigilant. We need to hold the ego at bay by committing to our daily practices and routine. A wise Guru or Spiritual mentor can be very helpful and beneficial in the beginning of our journey to provide guidance and assist us in avoiding all the pitfalls that are so common to beginners on the awakening path. Working with a Guru or mentor who is not qualified to guide us, is like the blind leading the blind. We need the guidance of someone who has already experienced what we want to experience. For example, a Guru who has never experienced Samadhi and/or some degree of Self-Realization is not qualified to guide us to our ultimate goal of Enlightenment.

Even for those who are steadfast on the awakening path in the beginning, it is possible to revert back to former states of apathy or laziness after a few months or years. However, we never lose the beneficial karma that we have accrued through our sadhana. Every time we sit to meditate, we plant positive samskaras in our Being, and we can always return when we are ready to re-commit to our practices. My own discipline has waxed and waned over the years, but I find that my resolve is the strongest when I am inspired. Inspiration on the path to Enlightenment can come in a myriad of forms. We may find inspiration by spending time in beautiful natural settings, being in the presence of the Guru, reading the Divinely inspired writings of the Masters, or attending meditation retreats. Therefore, as part of our Spiritual discipline, it is recommended to do all of the above as often as possible so that we may remain in a state of constant inspiration.

As part of my daily routine, I read Enlightened scripture, usually the writings of my Guru and Paramahansa Yogananda. I also occasionally peruse Patanjali's Yoga Sutras and the Bhagavad Gita. Other inspirational texts for yogis may include selections from the Upanishads, and Hatha Yoga texts like the Hatha Yoga Pradipika and Shiva Samhita. As yogis, if we choose to read texts outside of our tradition, we must use extreme discernment, or viveka, because it is very easy to become confused when mixing systems. This creates "mental indigestion" or intellectual confusion and should be avoided. It is also important that we do not over-read and clutter our minds with too many complicated metaphysical concepts. Meditation ought to be the priority. The first piece of advice Yogananda ever gave my Guru was, "Read a little, meditate more, and think of God all the time." Therefore, if we are meditating for thirty minutes every day, which should be the minimum time allotted, then perhaps twenty minutes of inspired reading is appropriate. If we wish to accelerate our Spiritual growth, then we should extend the duration of both our meditations and our scriptural study.

In the Yoga Sutras, Patanjali states that our rate of Spiritual growth is in direct proportion to the level of intensity of our sadhana. For example, people often ask me how long they should be meditating, and I respond by asking them how soon they would like to be Enlightened. For beginners or those with a limited amount of time in their schedule to devote to Spiritual practices, thirty minutes of meditation once a day is sufficient. However, as most people will find with practice, thirty minutes is usually not enough time to venture into superconscious territory. For serious yogis intent on awakening more quickly, forty five minutes to one hour once a day is recommended for the purpose of experiencing more prolonged superconscious states. For the most serious yogis, meditating twice a day for one hour each session is advisable. When I am being very disciplined and I sit for one hour twice a day, my realizations and insights are profound and I can sense a clear acceleration of my Enlightenment process. I have heard many Masters say that in order to achieve Enlightenment we need to sit for three hours a day usually in the early morning. This, of course, is not possible for most householders. However, I always find it interesting that my students without jobs or duties complain about a lack of Spiritual progress and when I ask them how much time they are devoting to meditation each day, they respond by saying they are only meditating for thirty minutes. The rest of their day is spent on social media, watching television, hanging out with friends and family, and finding other ways to waste time and energy. If one does not have a job or many worldly duties, then obviously two hours a day of meditation should be easy.

Roy Eugene Davis has awoken at around 3am in the morning and meditated for two to three hours consistently for almost seventy years. When he was young and living a monastic lifestyle he would meditate for more than five hours a day at times. Our level of intensity and devotion to our practices is a vital part of our Spiritual discipline. Each day is twenty four hours in length and most of us require around eight hours of restful sleep each night; this leaves sixteen hours spent in a waking state. If we spend two hours on pranayama and meditation each day, then that means we are devoting 12.5% of our day to experiencing higher states of consciousness. If we add to that Spiritual reading, prayer, chanting, or any other Spiritual practices, we might bring that percentage up to 20%. When put into perspective, we can see that 10-20% of our day spent in sadhana is not that much to ask, so I am always surprised by people who claim they do not even have thirty minutes a day to spend on meditation. Again, by eliminating non-essential activities from our daily schedule, we can rearrange our routine to accommodate our sadhana.

I was once told by a meditation teacher that spending more than two hours a day in meditation was for monks and was not advisable for householders. There have been times in my life when the intensity of my practice was very high and I was meditating for upwards of three hours a day. During these times, I had urges to leave the world behind and become a renunciate monk. However, I have family duties and work obligations that prevent me from adopting that type of lifestyle, and I feel as though it is not necessarily my dharma and karma to be a monk. I decided to lower my intensity level and cut back on the durations of my meditations to live a more balanced lifestyle as a householder. We must always be careful to maintain balance in our lives, especially as householders. In a recent meeting with my Guru he said, "We need to be somewhere in between heaven and Earth." This was in reference to some ecstatic Samadhi states during which I could not function and perform normal human activities. He was wisely expressing the need to maintain balance somewhere in between ecstasy and a functional, superconscious state of being.

There have been a few rare cases of advanced yogis who were in such an elevated state of Samadhi that they were unable to perform normal functions such as eating. They were so out of it that they could not even feed themselves or walk unattended. They required around the clock supervision and assistants. There is such a thing as too much. I once visited a famous Indian Guru and asked him about meditating too much and he said there is no such thing. He, of course, was a renunciate and always had been, and therefore had never had to perform normal duties and responsibilities. For him, perhaps there is no such thing as too much, but for a householder who is responsible for making the world go around, there most assuredly is such a thing as too much.

The ultimate goal of a disciplined, daily meditation practice is to maintain a superconscious state at all times, not just while we are meditating. That is why meditating twice a day is advisable because we prepare our consciousness in the morning and in the evening, and it becomes easier to sustain superconscious states and even lower levels of Samadhi throughout our normal daily activities. Lahiri Mahasaya, the founder of modern Kriya Yoga explains it as follows:

> Restless flows of prana cause mental restlessness. When the truth seeker is established in superconsciousness, meditation practice is natural and spontaneous. Then, even when one is not meditating, its benefits are enjoyed.

Attempting to maintain advanced Samadhi states at all times is not necessary or advisable for a householder and can cause us to completely withdraw from social and family obligations and duties. However, during our meditation practice and during prolonged meditation retreats, we are free to enjoy Samadhi ecstasy. Especially for householders, we must find a balance between our sadhana and our daily duties and responsibilities. It is completely possible to be superconscious and perform normal duties and activities. This ought to be the goal for householder yogis intent on experiencing Enlightenment and maintaining a lively and rich worldly life. During our meditation practice, we are free to dive as deep as we would like, but during our daily activities and interactions with people, we do not want to be "out of it" or otherworldly.

We have to be able to function here on planet Earth while we are incarnated in physical bodies. As yogis, we must strike a delicate balance between Spiritual ecstasy and our worldly affairs. This is why it is important to slowly acclimate ourselves back into our worldly activities after a meditation retreat. For many, this can be a jarring experience. One should ease their way back into their normal affairs following a meditation retreat. It is typically a good idea to give ourselves a day or two after the retreat before we integrate back into our duties and responsibilities. Likewise, it is a good idea to give ourselves an hour or so after our daily meditation practice before we begin our work-day, for example, to allow time for the assimilation of superconscious influences in the body and mind.

I have experienced deep states of Oneness during which I was unable to walk or function normally. This dysfunctional state subsides after a few hours, and I am again able to function in a normal manner. To be honest, while these states are pleasurable and transformative, I have no desire to remain in these states for extended periods of time due to the simple fact that I must perform my duties in the world. For renunciate yogis, prolonged states of Samadhi-ecstasy are not as disruptive to their lifestyle. It is important to mention at this point that ecstasy is not to be confused with bliss or ananda. Bliss is a preliminary phase experienced during precursory superconscious states and should be transcended. When my Guru once asked Yogananda how many of the saints and sages that he knew were fully Liberated, he responded by saying, "Not many. Most people are content with the bliss of God-communion." When we are experiencing bliss, there is still a subject (self) that is experiencing an object (bliss). During Samadhi, there is no separation between subject and object; there is only a Oneness that is beyond description. It is like the material (Shakti or Divine feminine) becomes aware of the Spiritual (Shiva or Divine masculine) and the Spiritual becomes aware of the material and they realize together instantaneously that they are One and the same. During Samadhi there is knowledge that all is Infinite Consciousness, even "material" objects, but even these descriptions do not even begin to describe the experience of Oneness. Samadhi is therefore something that must be experienced in one's Being and it cannot be understood intellectually or even intuitively.

There are several levels or types of Samadhi discussed by Patanjali in the Yoga Sutras, but the two primary types are Samadhi with support, and the more exalted state of Samadhi without support. An example of Samadhi with support is the experience of being in a very high, thought-free superconscious state with our focus completely on the inner light that is often visible during meditation. When our concentration becomes solely focused on this inner light and we have the sense that we are one with the light and there is no otherness, we are experiencing a Oneness with an object of contemplation or object of support. A higher form of Samadhi occurs when we experience a Oneness without an object of support or concentration and we are completely at one with our true nature, which is Unbounded, Infinite Consciousness.

For clarification, the stages of Enlightenment are as follows:

Ego-consciousness - In this state of consciousness we are identified with our false, limited ego-self. In a state of ego-consciousness we are unable to sever our identification from the body/mind/personality composite and we are subject to the ignorance and suffering implicit in ego-identity. In this state of being, we lack self-control and self-awareness and are completely mired in the illusion of maya.

Witness-consciousness - In this state of consciousness, we are just beginning the awakening process and we are able to step outside of ourselves to witness thoughts, emotions, reactions, memories, desires, habit-patterns, etc...The Buddhists mistakenly refer to this stage of development as "mindfulness" even though the mind has nothing to do with it. It is the consciousness, which is witnessing the mind and its contents. In this stage, we begin to sever our identity with the false ego-self experiencing a shift of perspective. We realize that if it is possible to witness the mind and its inner workings then we must be other than the mind. Most people with very little practice can experience being the witness, and this is why "mindfulness" training has become so popular and is even taught in the offices of large corporations.

Superconsciousness mixed with thoughts and perceptions - In this state, our consciousness is superior to ordinary states of consciousness, but it is still mixed at times with thoughts, emotions, desires, memories, and perceptions that momentarily distract our attention. During this stage, we are beginning to see the possibility of experiencing clear, thought-free states, but our attention may continue to occasionally wander and become distracted by vrittis, or fluctuations within our Being.

Superconsciousness- In this stage of development, we are able to witness all finite phenomenon with dispassionate objectivity in a reactionless state of tranquil soul-peace. This state of consciousness is similar in some ways to witness-consciousness, but it is a thought free state where our awareness if far more focused and objective. Our identity begins to loosen in this stage and our misidentification with the ego is weakened, but there is still some sense of individual existence. It is during this stage that the physical and energetic benefits of meditation begin to occur. The brain may begin to produce soma nectar, which can be tasted as a special form of saliva in the mouth. This soma makes its way into the rest of our system and becomes amrita, which has a nourishing and enlivening effect. We may begin to notice the om vibration as a subtle sound current in and around the head and see a brilliant inner light in the Spiritual eye center. This light is usually white, but can appear as purple, blue, and gold at various times depending on the state of our nervous system and our particular stage of development. The physical immune system is improved and the intellect becomes more refined and discerning. We can remain in this state as we go about our normal daily routine remaining as an objective observer in all circumstances.

Samadhi with support - During this type of Samadhi, we experience union with an object of contemplation. For example, we may experience the complete union of our attention and awareness with the om vibration or the inner light during meditation. This type of Samadhi is beneficial, but is not the highest state of realization. While it provides the yogi with a taste of union, it is but a precursor to the Divine Union that is experienced during Samadhi without support.

Samadhi without support - During Samadhi without support, we are in complete Divine Union. There is no separateness. This experience is ineffable, or beyond description; words simply do not do it justice. In Samadhi, there is no sense of independence or individuality and identification with ego is non-existent. Samadhi experiences are temporary and therefore, are not the ultimate goal of our practice. The experience is transformative, but not lasting. We require many Samadhi experiences before our consciousness and Being becomes so clear that Oneness and Self-knowing is permanent.

Self-Realization - In this stage of Enlightenment, we are in a permanent state of Self-knowing and never return to former states of ordinary, ego-based consciousness. We experience complete realization of the Self, or soul, and there is no longer any confusion about what we are. Even the Self-Realized must still work out remaining karma and continue to clean up the subconscious layer of the mind, but they do not accrue any new karma because they are no longer identified with the false-self, which is subject to karma. Siddhis, or supernatural powers and abilities, may be acquired during this stage.

God-Realization - In this stage of Enlightenment, the unmanifest aspect and the manifest aspect of God are known and fully understood. The processes of cosmic manifestation are grasped and there are no further questions in the mind of the yogi; all is known. Siddhis may increase during this stage as the body of the yogi becomes more and more Spiritualized.

Liberation - This is the final or ultimate stage of Enlightenment. Very few Masters reach this final stage, but it is possible to achieve during one incarnation with diligent, concentrated endeavor. For one who is liberated, all karma has been transcended and neutralized. This state of being is desire-free and there is no possibility of suffering. It is a state of total Spiritual freedom. Siddhis are fully developed. There is no need for Liberated Masters to reincarnate on a physical planet. They many continue their work on astral and causal planes or manifest physical bodies at will in order to work with small groups of advanced yogis in secluded places; Mahavatar Babaji, the Guru of Lahiri Mahasaya, is one example of such a being.

5 LIFESTYLE

"Forget the past. The vanished lives of all men are dark with many shames. Human conduct is ever unreliable until man is anchored in the Divine. Everything in the future will improve if you are making a spiritual effort now."
-Sri Yukteswar

The era in which the Yoga Sutras was composed was a philosophy-rich period in the history of India. During this period there were six main schools of orthodox philosophy deriving from Ancient India: Samkhya, Yoga, Vaisheshika, Nyaya, Mimamsa, and Vedanta. Along with the orthodox schools, there were also two unorthodox schools: Buddhism and Jainism. Some scholars assert that Patanjali's Yoga Sutras was, in essence, a response to the Buddhist philosophy that was sweeping India at the time of its composition. The Yoga Sutras also contain portions of other systems of thought that complemented the philosophy of Yoga at the time, such as Samkhya.

In the Samkhya system of philosophy we find the cosmology of the three gunas, or constituent attributes of nature. Samkhya is a dualistic philosophy that divides Reality into Spirit (Purusha) and matter (Prakriti). The gunas can be thought of as the three fundamental influences in manifestation, or Prakriti. The combination and interaction of the three gunas determines the characteristics of someone or something. Tamas guna is the densifying influence in nature and can be thought of as the glue that holds the universe together. Rajas guna is the activating influence in nature and is responsible for change and activity. Sattva guna is the elevating influence in nature and is responsible for lightness and illumination.

We can also think about the gunas in terms of vibration and frequency. Through modern physics, we know that everything in the universe is vibration and that every object in the universe produces a specific frequency. Taking this a step further, there is even mounting evidence that every object in the universe is produced *by* a specific frequency. We can think of tamas guna as the influence that lowers vibrational frequency, rajas guna as the influence that changes vibrational frequency, and sattva guna as the influence that raises vibrational frequency. Many recent experiments have been done proving that human emotions and energy can affect water and plants and other objects that were previously thought of as "unconscious." These experiments demonstrate the relationship between our energetic vibration and the energetic vibration of objects in nature. Our vibrational frequency has a definitive effect on the frequency of the surrounding environment. We can influence it in a positive or negative manner depending upon our current state of being. Likewise, the frequencies within a particular environment have an effect on our frequency as well. All is interconnected in a spectrum of energetic vibrations, frequencies, and harmonics.

When we make lifestyle choices as yogis, we should always choose the most sattvic option. It is this simple rule of thumb that can simplify our lifestyle choices and make the decision making process far less complicated. For example, when confronted with any decision, we can simply ask ourselves which option is the most elevating and illuminating and choose accordingly. This certainly simplifies matters and allows us to base our decisions upon which choice will raise the vibrational frequency of our Being the most, leading to a sattvic state. Tamasic choices leave us more dense and identified with ego, whereas sattvic choices leave us more elevated and less identified with ego.

An easy illustration of a lifestyle choice that we must all make is choosing foods that promote a yogic way of life. The Hatha Yoga Pradipika has a list of foods that are deemed to be sattvic by the author, Swami Svatmarama. This list of foods suitable for yogis includes wheat, rice, ghee, moong, green vegetables, honey, ginger, etc... There are other yogic texts that include food lists for yogis, but all the lists are comprised exclusively of vegetarian foods. All yogic texts, as well as Yoga Gurus, recommend a vegetarian diet (with the exception of a few groups of tantric yogis who eat meat). Therefore, within the Yoga community, a vegetarian diet is by far the most common and agreed upon diet for yogis.

With all that we currently know regarding the health and environmental benefits of a vegetarian diet, it seems the obvious choice for everyone on the planet. However, meat is a sense pleasure that many find difficult to overcome. For anyone serious about Enlightenment, it is advisable to transcend the carnal desire to eat flesh and to begin adhering to a strict vegetarian or vegan diet. Meat is a dense, tamasic substance that weighs us down physically and energetically and should be avoided. The vast majority of farm animals live in deplorable conditions and are not treated with compassion and respect. I am always surprised by people I meet who own several dogs and consider themselves animal lovers, but continue to eat pork and beef thereby supporting the slaughter industry.

I was staying with some friends one time on their newly acquired farm. They had decided to become cattle ranchers after years spent as vegetarians, which was odd in and of itself. During my visit, we had a conversation about how the cows were treated. My friends explained to me that the cows were "treated like part of the family" and that they were handled in a very humane fashion. I then asked how the cows were killed when it was time to process them for meat. My friend responded by saying that he shot them in the head with a shotgun. I am unaware of anyone who treats their family in such a way.

Mammals care for their young and are capable of experiencing a wide range of emotions, including love. When they are murdered, they release a nasty cocktail of hormones and chemicals into their system associated with panic and fear. When we consume the meat of a murdered animal, we ingest their panic and fear. For a yogi intent on Self-Realization, ingesting the negative vibrations associated with the act of killing is not helpful. There are some Gurus who even believe that we accrue negative karma when we eat meat. What can be said for certain is that meat eating does not conform to the practice of ahimsa, or nonviolence.

The idea that we need to eat meat to stay strong and get an adequate amount of protein in our diet is a fallacy. There are many seeds, nuts, beans, and grains that possess large amounts of protein. I have spoken to many deluded individuals who justify their addiction to meat by stating that they have a certain blood type that actually requires the consumption of animal flesh. A quick Internet search reveals that the blood type diet is not based on any scientifically valid evidence and that, in fact, the opposite is true. All of the scientific studies that have been conducted with regards to the blood type diet have found that there is absolutely no empirical validity to the diet and that it is a completely hollow theory that someone invented to sell books. Often times, making a mature decision to leave something behind that we know is wrong is not easy. It requires will, determination, and the ability to set the ego and its desires aside for the good of the whole.

Depending on which study one looks at, vegetarians and vegans have an increased life expectancy of five to fifteen years. For one on the Enlightenment path, a long, healthy life is of great benefit. The longer we are embodied, the longer we have to work toward our Spiritual evolution and our ultimate aim of Liberation. There are many recorded cases of yogis living well past one hundred years old. The Shivapuri Baba, for instance, lived to be one hundred and thirty seven years old. Lokenath and other advanced yogis allegedly lived beyond the age of one hundred and fifty. What we might deem impossible for an ordinary human is arbitrary when considering what is possible for a yogi to accomplish. Not only does living a long life enable us to work on our own Spiritual Enlightenment, but it also allows us to help others on their paths as well. There have been teachers from traditions such as Jainism who think that the Earth is evil and dirty and that long life is not necessarily desirable. I find this type of philosophy to be life-negating and ignorant. Once someone experiences Samadhi, any idea of the separation of material and Spiritual life is sophomoric.

Mankind's lust for meat is having a devastating impact on the global environment and human health. There are many recent studies revealing a strong correlation between cancer rates and animal protein consumption by Dr. Colin Campbell and others. Animal products, in this context, include dairy and eggs. A clean, organic, vegan diet is ideal for a yogi. There is no need to be a fanatic with our diet however. For example, if someone at a dinner party offers us something that we would not normally eat, we can be polite and taste it. There is no need to make a scene and preach to our friends or family about the immorality of meat. This type of egotistical display of moral superiority is possibly more immature than the consumption of meat itself. As yogis, we always want to be humble and modest with our opinions and lifestyle choices. Judging others for their choices is self-defeating and counterproductive on the Spiritual path. Strong identification with opinions strengthens our sense of self; the goal of the Spiritual path is to weaken our sense of self.

A simple experiment can be done to determine the different energetic qualities of foods. After one eats a meal, they can sit still for a few minutes and inwardly feel the after-effects of specific foods. For those whose nervous system is dull due to the use of drugs or over-stimulation of the senses, this will be difficult. However, as we improve our inner sensitivity and refine our nervous system, we can easily discern which foods are sattvic, rajasic, and tamasic. Sattvic foods leave us feeling light and elevated. Rajasic foods leave us feeling restless and agitated. Tamasic foods leave us feeling dull, sleepy, and weighed down.

Examples of sattvic foods include leafy greens, ripe fruits, seeds, lightly cooked vegetables, and most grains. Rajasic foods include chocolate, caffeine, garlic, peppers, and any foods that are over-spiced. Meat, cheese, bread, fried foods, and sweets are examples of tamasic foods that should be avoided. Depending on where one lives, gaining access to organic, sattvic foods might be more difficult. For instance, when I first moved to Chile, I immediately noticed that the normal Chilean diet was incredibly tamasic, full of meat, cheese, fried foods, white bread, and gratuitous amounts of alcohol. However, over time, I discovered the stores and restaurants that served healthy, sattvic food. I even discovered that there is a sizeable vegetarian population here in Chile. If we are determined to eat healthy, we can find options no matter where we live and no matter what the predominant social norms might be.

When we are making dietary choices, it is also important to have a basic understanding of the principles of Ayurveda. Ayurveda is an ancient Indian system of medicine based upon the idea of the three doshas. The doshas can be thought of as basic body-mind constitutions. The vast majority of us have a dominant dosha that determines our physical, mental, and personality characteristics. Pitta dosha is a combination of the fire and water elements and expresses in the body as heat and digestive fluids. Vata dosha is a combination of air and ether and expresses in the body as breath and gasses. Kapha dosha is a combination of earth and water and expresses in the body as fat and mucus. This is a gross over simplification of the doshas, but it is well beyond the scope of this book. I recommend reading any of the books by Dr. Vasant Lad on the subject for more information.

Our choice of foods should correspond to our dominant dosha to achieve optimum health. For example, someone with a pitta dominance should avoid hot, spicy foods that aggravate pitta, which can lead to digestive issues and anger. Vata types should limit the amount of gas causing foods that they consume in an effort to avoid bloating and anxiety. Kapha types should avoid heavy, fattening foods to avoid weight gain and feelings of inertia. There are many excellent books and websites that offer food lists for each dosha. By following the guidelines of an Ayurvedic diet plan, we can limit the amount of physical and emotional problems that might arise otherwise. Eating merely for taste and personal preference is a sign of emotional immaturity and should be transcended. Food should be thought of as medicine and fuel. There is nothing wrong with enjoying a meal, but not at the expense of our health or the health of the planet.

Another lifestyle choice that we are faced with on a regular basis concerns what kind of media or entertainment to consume. We should follow the same guidelines when choosing our entertainment that we use when choosing food and always choose the most sattvic options. Mainstream news, most Hollywood movies, violent video games, and social media all have a tamasic quality. If we are able to consume media and entertainment in moderation, then a small daily dose is tolerable for yogis. However, I know many people who spend almost their entire day on social media, texting on their phone, watching television, and playing video games and then complain that they have great difficulty meditating. Over stimulation of the senses should be guarded against if we wish to calm and refine the brain and nervous system. There is a reason that the ancient yogis spent time in nature and limited their amount of sensory input. A few hours spent alone inside a cave will tell us all we need to know about the difference between an environment of sensory overload versus an environment of stillness meant for the practice of pratyahara. The Shvetashvatara Upanishad gives a beautiful description of the ideal environment in which to spend our time:

> In a clean level spot, free from pebbles, fire and gravel,
> Delightful by its sounds, its water and bowers,
> Favorable to thought, not offensive to the eye,
> In a hidden retreat protected from the wind,
> One should practice Yoga.

We can perform the same experiment with our entertainment options that we perform with food. For example, after we watch a movie, we can sit in the silence for a few minutes and dive inward. Do we feel uplifted and light (sattvic)? Do we feel agitated (rajasic)? Or, do we feel heavy (tamasic)? Our inner state of being is a clear indicator that allows us to gauge which movies or video games or apps we should spend our time consuming.

For the purposes of detoxifying our senses, occasional meditation retreats are essential. During a retreat, we can turn inward and spend a few days without sensory stimulus. Personally, I spend far too much time on the Internet doing research, reading news, watching Youtube videos, sending emails, checking social media, and generally wasting time. I take advantage of the time I spend at meditation retreats and I commit to be device-free for a few days. I feel amazingly refreshed and renewed after a few days spent without any screen time. For the last few years, I have gone without using a cell phone except for emergencies and it has made a difference in my lifestyle and the way I feel. The link between cell phone use and brain cancer is undeniable, and yogis should sincerely reflect over their use of cell phones and other electronic devices.

Another lifestyle choice that presents itself in the life of a yogi is how much to exercise. We must also make decisions regarding the best manner in which to exercise; this includes our asana practice. The way in which one practices asana is an explicit determining factor in their level of Spiritual maturity. For those yogis who practice asana exclusively without including pranayama, mantra, meditation, and other higher practices of Yoga, yogi is not a term that they ought to be misusing to describe themselves. This is especially true for those who practice asana in a competitive manner. The Hatha Yogis who invented many of our modern postures did not intend to create a practice for people to compete with each other to see who can do the fanciest posture and look good in a pair of Yoga pants. I do not mean to generalize and stereotype, but unfortunately, this is what has become of the predominate "Yoga" community in the West.

Mild to moderate exercise is a vital part of the daily routine of a yogi concerned with physical and mental health. Without a properly functioning body, Enlightenment is far more difficult to unveil. Again, the body is a Divine template of awakening and must be treated with care. However, many people take exercise to the extreme and engage in exercise routines that put far too much strain on muscles, bones, and joints that, over time, cause unnecessary wear and tear on the body. For example, extreme weight lifting and running will cause more harm than good in the long term. Swimming, walking, moderate Vinyasa Yoga, cycling, and other resistance based routines are far safer and produce less physical strain than most of the work-outs that are so popular right now like Crossfit, long distance running, weight lifting, mixed-martial arts, etc...

The way that most people approach Yoga asana in the West is clearly based in body-consciousness. The pressure to look a certain way, especially for women, has guided the direction that asana classes have taken in the West. The popularization of Yoga by Hollywood celebrities has had both positive and negative consequences. On the one hand, it has exposed many people to Yoga that would not have otherwise been exposed, but on the other hand, it has created the image of Yoga as a physical workout meant to sculpt and tone the bodies of insecure women wishing to look like the celebrities that they worship and adore. While Yoga asana can create the type of body that is very appealing to the superficial male, this was never the intent. I am obviously not a woman, and I can only imagine what it must be like to exist in a world where every detail of a female's body is scrutinized and evaluated by men, as well as other women. I empathize with women's obsession with looking perfect like the models on magazine covers and the actresses in movies. However, this obsession with physical perfection is corrupting the original intent and purpose of Yoga and it has created a false image of what a yogi is in our culture. Many people think that a yogi is an attractive woman with a perfect body wearing skin-tight, revealing clothes who is abnormally flexible and comes from a predominantly upper-middle class background. This is the common image that most Westerners have as it concerns what a practitioner of Yoga looks like.

Yoga asana should be practiced in a meditative mood, with loose fitting, comfortable clothing in an atmosphere of cooperation, rather than competition. Women who show off their bodies by wearing next to nothing in Yoga studios do a disservice to men that are trying to concentrate in a class, Yoga itself, and themselves. Engaging in an ego-based competition with others in a Yoga class is childish and immature and has no place in the world of Yoga. In fact, once one has mastered a few key postures and sun salutations, there is really no need to practice with others in a Yoga studio or gym. Yoga is better practiced alone in one's home. With the availability of free, high quality videos on the Internet, practicing at home is far easier than ever before. There is nothing wrong with attending an occasional class in a studio or gym, especially to learn new asanas or new styles of Yoga, but we must introspect and ask ourselves why we have the need to practice in a studio. Is it because we genuinely need help with our asanas, or is it because we like to be seen by others? Is it because we are truly interested in learning, or is it because we want others to notice how much we have progressed and show off? It is because we want to have the instruction of a quality yoga teacher, or is it because we are dependent upon the community found at the studio?

There is a sad trend occurring in the world of Yoga today regarding the posting of photos of oneself doing asanas on social media. I cannot think of a more obvious way to demonstrate one's Spiritual immaturity and ego-based consciousness. I can understand the desire to post a picture or two of oneself doing a posture in a beautiful setting to share with friends and family, but there are people that have entire Instagram accounts completely devoted to showing off their bodies posed in various asanas with literally hundreds of photos. What is even more appalling is that these people seem to have hundreds or even thousands of followers who condone and encourage this type of behavior without hesitation. In fact, there are many yogis who spend countless hours on social media subtly competing with each other to do the most advanced posture in the most interesting setting possible.

The practice of Yoga asana is meant to lead us away from body-consciousness. However, in the West, Yoga asana has become a way to promote body-consciousness and identification with our temporary vessel. It is this trend that needs to be reversed so that we can restore Yoga back to its original intent and purpose. Yoga instructors should be educating their students about the higher practices of pranayama, mantra, meditation, and Samadhi, not just asana. Yoga instructors should also discourage competition in their classes and showing up to class scantily clad. Some more conservative Yoga traditions actually have a dress code that must be followed by both men and women in Yoga classes. In the past, I would have cringed at such a notion, but I now realize the wisdom inherent in these customs. In a Yoga class, we are not there to show off our body parts and tempt members of the opposite sex like dogs in heat; we are there to prepare our bodies for meditation and higher states of consciousness.

The doshas also come into play when deciding what type of Yoga or exercise routine to adopt. For pitta types, competitive sports should be avoided. Slow, meditative, non-competitive Yoga is best for people with a dominant pitta dosha. Hot Yoga and Ashtanga Yoga are antithetical to the balancing of pitta dosha in the body. For vata types, styles of Yoga that require longer holds of postures like Iyengar are advisable to promote concentration and stillness. For Kapha types, intense cardiovascular workouts are highly beneficial for burning calories, and a vigorous Vinyasa Yoga class that requires a great deal of movement is also recommended. For more information on which style of Yoga is best for each dosha, I recommend reading <u>Yoga for Your Type</u>, by David Frawley.

Depending upon our dosha, twenty to thirty minutes of mild aerobic exercise every day is sufficient for maintaining optimum health. We need not do the same exercise every day. We may decide to swim once a week, do an asana class three times a week, and go for a brisk walk the other three days. As long as we are moving our bodies on a daily basis and getting our heart rate up for twenty to thirty minutes, we need not worry about doing more unless we are severely overweight. Regular exercise boosts our immune system, improves digestion, relieves stress, improves mood, and helps us sleep. Over the years, I have noticed that when I am exercising regularly, my sleep is much better, which leads to better meditations in the morning.

Adequate sleep is of the utmost importance on the awakening path. We do not want to be sleep deprived and in a mental fog when we are trying to meditate. Most people require between seven to nine hours of deep, restful sleep each night. There are advanced yogis who only sleep two or three hours at night because they meditate for long hours during the day and their bodies do not require the same amount of rest, but for the average householder yogi, at least seven hours a night is advisable. We should cooperate with the cycles of nature and go to bed shortly after the sun sets and wake up shortly after sunrise or even before sunrise.

There is a special, rarified energy that occurs just before sunrise that yogis should take advantage of. During this time, the rest of the world, including the animal kingdom, is still asleep and there is a peace that pervades nature that yogis can partake of when they meditate at this hour. Even if we consider ourselves to be "night people" and have trouble falling asleep early, with practice and training, we can adapt ourselves to the cycles of nature. Staying up late to socialize or watch television when we know we are supposed to get up early to meditate is an act of Spiritual immaturity. We must sacrifice the desires of the lower self to attain the exalted Union with our higher Self. Many people report that they have difficulty waking up early to meditate and when I ask them what time they go to bed at night, they often tell me that they go to bed after midnight. Staying up this late is not natural and it disrupts the natural circadian rhythms of the body. Nine or ten o'clock is a good time for a yogi to retire. Five or six o'clock in the morning is a reasonable time to wake up and meditate, although there are many yogis who wake up at two or three in the morning to do their sadhana.

The amount of social interaction that we engage in is another lifestyle choice that we must confront as yogis. I hear from many people that they are "extraverts" and they require almost constant social interaction to feel normal. These extraverted people have their attention outwardly focused nearly all the time and are unceasingly engaged in social interaction via social functions, meetings, talking by phone, texting, emailing, and using social media. They never give themselves the time for quiet self reflection and the internalization of attention. I have noticed that it is generally far easier for introverted individuals to meditate. Enlightenment is possible for extraverts as well, but it seems as though they have to work much harder at it. For extraverts, finding time to be alone and reflect is essential. When our attention is constantly outwardly focused, we waste energy on non-essential conversations, gossip, small-talk, and social maneuvering that would be better spent focusing our attention inward on the essential matter of Spiritual awakening.

In order that we may simplify our social lives, maintaining relationships with two or three close friends is sufficient. I was fortunate enough to spend some time in the presence of Sri Karunamayi (a female saint from India) and she mentioned that for a Spiritual seeker it is recommended to have only two or three close friends. I was still in my mid-twenties at the time and heavily involved in my social life and I had no idea why should she would even mention such a proposition. A life with only two or three friends sounded to me like social suicide. I did not understand the profound wisdom in her words during that period of my life, but as I have gotten older, I can see how limiting social interaction is vital for the simplification of life that is necessary for one on the Spiritual Enlightenment path. The more friendships that we have to maintain and nurture, the more distractions we will have in our lives.

I have noticed that friends come and go, and that we attempt to hold on to friendships only to realize that circumstances change, personalities change, people move, and that very seldom do we maintain lifelong friendships with people. When I was in college, I had close friends that I thought I would have for the rest of my life and I rarely have contact with any of them now. Also, when I was in my mid-twenties and began meditating regularly, I stopped spending time with the majority of the friends that I had during that period of my life. We find that as our Spiritual unfoldment continues to evolve, we no longer have an interest in spending time with people that we used to be close to, especially if they are not on a similar Spiritual trajectory. This is natural and normal and should not be resisted.

Our false identity is largely shaped and molded through the process of social interaction. As pack animals, we are instinctively driven to fit in to a particular subgroup and/or society as a whole. This desire for a sense of belonging is one of our most primal urges that we have as human beings. When we are on auto-pilot and sleepwalking through life, we base many of our decisions on whether or not the people around us will accept us and our choices. For example, many unconscious people follow a particular religion not because it makes sense, but out of fear of ostracization from their subgroup. If people possessed the capability to step outside of their social self and view their irrational beliefs from an objective perspective, they would suddenly realize how absurd many of their beliefs are. However, the need for acceptance trumps reason and logic and people continue to live their lives in a dream-like state, unaware that they are living a socially conditioned existence.

What we typically think of as the false self is actually our social self. It is an illusory mental construct created out of the need to survive within a tribal grouping in a state of nature. There is a fear hardwired into us that tells us we might not survive if we are not accepted by our subgroup, which includes family and friends (the tribe). If we dress and act a certain way, we fear that our subgroup will not accept us, and thousands of years ago, this meant that we might not have access to food and potential mates. The need to belong was natural and necessary for our survival within tribal systems of the ancient past.

Our personality is not really chosen consciously by us, but by those around us. Most of the things we like and dislike are not based upon conscious choices, but instead are based upon the messages that members of our subgroup send us regarding our choices. The music we listen to, the clothes we wear, the hobbies we have, our interests, our political beliefs, and our religious beliefs are largely based upon what others would think of us if we did not have these interests and beliefs. Our personality is fear based. It is shaped by how the "other" views the self. When we begin to wake up from the dream, one of the first things that we realize is that we have been living our lives for someone else. We realize that we have been making choices based upon our fear of being left out, rather than consciously choosing our interests, beliefs, and lifestyle.

Even for people on a Spiritual awakening path, the temptation to feel a sense of belonging persists. There are many people who join churches, Guru-cults, organizations, and groups because they yearn for a sense of belonging. People think that because they belong to a "Spiritual" organization that the same rules of social engagement do not apply. However, once involved in an organization, we quickly find that there is the same propensity to want to fit in and belong. We worry about how others will view us if we behave or act a certain way. We begin to change the way we dress, the music we listen to, our interests and hobbies, and even the words and vocabulary that we use in an attempt to fit in and feel accepted by our new subgroup, and we ultimately fall back into the same patterns of personality-building in a new setting with a new group of people. Even though I belong to a Spiritual organization, I find it best to limit my interaction with the other people within the organization as much as possible. My Guru, when told by members of our organization that they do not have anyone else in the organization living near them, he replies by saying partly in jest, "You're lucky." Mr. Davis also encourages retreat participants at CSA to limit their social interaction during retreats to focus on the matter at hand.

There is no need to be anti-social on the Spiritual path. Yogis can live a perfectly normal life in the world and interact with others in an ordinary manner. However, as yogis, we should limit our amount of social interaction and avoid situations where people are discussing controversial topics that might trigger our ego to react. When we engage in arguments or debates with others, the ego feels threatened and engages in a competition, believing that if it can only prove that it is right and the person is wrong, then it will somehow win. We never win with ego. Every time we are identified with ego, we lose Spiritually. The need to be right is a sign of emotional and Spiritual immaturity and should be overcome and transcended as quickly as possible for one on the Enlightenment path. When the ego is proven wrong, it again fears ostracization from the subgroup and a loss of social status. When the ego is proven right, we experience a little ego-buzz and feel as though our social status and intelligence has been affirmed, procuring a secure place within the social hierarchy of our subgroup. This ego-buzz, like all highs, wears off and we search out other situations in which we can engage in frivolous debate with others so that we can prove our self worth again. When viewed objectively, we can see just how silly this cycle truly is.

For a Western yogi on the path of Spiritual unfoldment, dressing up like an Indian Sadhu to impress others is completely unnecessary. There is a trend in the West for so called yogis to wear dreadlocks, grow a beard, wear beads, and get Sanskrit tattoos all over their bodies to draw attention to themselves and appear as "real yogis." Our outer appearance has nothing to do with our inner experience or level of consciousness. It is unnecessary to dramatize our lifestyle to the rest of the world in an attempt to show off. In fact, doing so can be a great obstacle on the path, as we become so body-conscious and concerned with how we are perceived by others, that we forget the actual purpose of Yoga and meditation. If we want to wear some Indian clothes for special occasions like initiation services or homa fire ceremonies, there is nothing wrong with that, but we need not look like an Indian person all the time to practice Yoga and meditation successfully. Many modern female yogis likewise treat Yoga as though it were a Madison Avenue fashion trend and not a Spiritual practice. There are huge corporations manufacturing Yoga clothes for women, and it has become quite the fad to walk around town with Yoga pants on carrying a fashionable Yoga mat bag. It seems as though there are many women who go to Yoga classes just so they can be seen walking down the street in their Yoga pants carrying their Yoga mats in an attempt to look cool and hip and fit in with their shallow friends.

Also, with regards to our outer appearance, it is best to cease our identification with race, ethnicity, class, religious background, and gender. Identification with these types of characteristics is antithetical to the awakening process. When we label ourselves categorically, we automatically separate ourselves from others, and strengthen and solidify the false self. To identify with anything finite is to live in Spiritual ignorance. It is wonderful to see the increase in inter-racial couples and the elimination of racial divisions happening the world over. We still have a long way to go, but things are certainly better than they have ever been in that regard. As humanity evolves, racial barriers will continue to diminish. Religious differences continue to plague the world as Muslims are pitted against Jews and Christians by the powers that be in an effort to destabilize the world using Machiavellian strategies for the purposes of increasing weapons sales and the procurement of oil. As yogis, adherence to antiquated belief systems and identification with organized religions should be transcended. Gender might be the most difficult human characteristic to overcome. From a very early age, we are conditioned to identify with our sex. However, even our identification with this limiting quality should be overcome. I have noticed during my time spent with Enlightened people that they possess masculine and feminine qualities in a near perfect balance.

The relationship that we have with money is another lifestyle choice that we must make as yogis. There is a common myth amongst many Spiritual seekers that they must live a life of poverty or austerity in order to experience Enlightenment. There is nothing about living in comfortable, abundant circumstances that prevents us from waking up. In fact, having a comfortable, financially abundant lifestyle can be of great benefit to those on a Spiritual path. I have met some yogis who are poor and use Spirituality as their excuse to remain poor instead of getting the education and skills they need to support themselves financially. Poverty should not be a hindrance to our Spiritual growth either, but it is certainly not necessary.

One time when I was driving down the highway that goes into Crestone, Colorado where I used to live, I picked up a hitchhiker (which is a common practice there). We engaged in a conversation and she told me that she preferred not having a car because it made her feel more "free" and that possessing objects only brings about bondage. This type of attitude is infantile and is common to those people who use inane Spiritual justifications to rationalize their inability to earn money in a mature fashion. What provides us with more freedom; owning our own vehicle and going wherever we want whenever we want, or constantly relying on others for rides? There is nothing wrong with possessing objects as long as we do not allow ourselves to become attached to them. The less identified we are with the false self, the less attached we are to the possessions of the false self. We need not lead a life of poverty to learn the lessons of non-attachment.

Avoiding debts from loans and credit cards is wise when attempting to simplify our lives. I know from personal experience the undue stress that financial debt can create in one's life. Until recently, saving money was very difficult for my wife and I, but we have managed to pay off debts and limit our spending and we can now live a life of financial freedom. We have also made some wise business decisions and investments that have paid off and we no longer worry as much about money. This type of financial freedom has allowed us more mental space for the pursuit of our Spiritual goals. When we are young and immature, we tend to spend money that we do not have and we take out loans and use credit cards to buy unnecessary items. As we get older, we learn that the temporary satisfaction associated with the purchase of a particular good or service is not worth the years that it takes to pay it off.

We can dive deep into the Infinite as yogis, and still maintain a comfortable material life for ourselves in the finite world. Taking on financial responsibility is a sign that we are growing to Spiritual and emotional maturity. If we are still relying on our parents or other relatives for our sustenance, then it is more difficult to grow emotionally and Spiritually. For instance, I have known many people who live off of trust funds and inheritances from their relatives. Because these people have never had to enter the workforce or earn money on their own, their emotional and Spiritual maturity is greatly stunted. These people seem to live in a fantasy world and they are completely out of touch with reality. They continue to live as spoiled children long into their adult years. There is certainly nothing wrong with accepting an inheritance from a loved one, but we should not allow it to make us lazy and complacent. I once told my Guru that I had taken a part time job so that I could focus more on my Spiritual practices and he said, "Now, we don't want to be lazy yogis." Even if we succeed in achieving financial success or inherit large amounts of money that allow us to live without the need to work, we should continue to fill our time with meaningful activities that benefit others and donate a portion of our funds to charitable organizations.

What we do for a living should benefit others and have a positive impact on humanity and the planet. As yogis, we should avoid careers that take advantage of people or that negatively exploit the resources of the planet. For instance, working at a restaurant that sells meat and alcohol demonstrates a lack of conscience on our behalf. Likewise, working for large transnational corporations that pollute the environment and/or take advantage of sweatshop labor should be eschewed. Also, it is advisable to avoid jobs that overtax and overstress the body and nervous system so that we are not too tired to do our Spiritual practices. For many years, I worked as a middle school teacher and found it incredibly difficult to find the energy to meditate after work. I came home exhausted every day and my Spiritual unfoldment suffered because of it. We must find a balance that works for us, and this balance will look different for everyone depending upon their particular occupation and work schedule. Most of all, it is best to discover what line of work is the most dharmic for us to do. When our work is dharmic, we feel as though we are in our right place in life doing exactly what we are supposed to be doing in an almost effortless manner. We are not victims of our circumstances, and we possess the free will to choose work that best suits our gifts and skills. If we do not yet possess the skills needed to pursue a compatible career, we can acquire those skills.

Whatever we do not yet have, we can attract and have. There is a technique that is part of the Kriya Yoga tradition known as "floating it in om." It is a type of prayer that we can use to attract useful events and circumstances into our lives. When have successfully meditated to a state of superconsciousness, we can merge our attention and awareness with the om vibration. We do not necessarily need to be in a Samadhi state where we are entirely at one with om, but we need to be superconscious and have our attention and awareness blended with om. We can begin listening for a subtle sound vibration happening in and around our head. This may start as an electrical sound or the sound of blood flowing in the head and brain. We should then go beyond this sound to an even more subtle sound current and so on and so forth until we feel as though we are immersed in the om vibration, which is the primordial sound of creation and is the substratum out of which the universe manifests. It is the closest we can get to the unmanifest Infinite in the manifest material realm. When we are entirely immersed in om, we can visualize what we want to have in our ajna chakra and float the object of our wholesome desire into om, and send it out in the universe and await its fulfillment. While we are visualizing the object or circumstance that we wish to manifest, we should have the feeling of already possessing that object in our Being.

The key to the law of attraction is the ability to be superconscious while visualizing our object of desire, floating it in om, and then having the feeling of already possessing that object. It is necessary to hold this feeling in our consciousness for a few minutes before concluding our meditation session. We can repeat this process on a daily basis until our wholesome desires are fulfilled. We can also use this procedure when we are contemplating something that we wish to know the answer to. For example, if we wish to know how the universe manifests itself out of an unmanifest field of Pure Consciousness, we can ask this question and float it in om and wait for an answer. Most people are surprised how quick and effective this method is. There is nothing magical about it. It is simply cause and effect and the universal law of attraction. Magic and magnet have the same root word and essentially mean the same thing. Magic is really just the ability to attract what we wish to have in our lives and to manifest thought-forms into this material dimension. We can do this using the method of floating it in om, but our results are best the more superconscious we are and the more wholesome our desires are.

As yogis, we may decide to begin teaching Yoga and meditation at some point along our journey. This is an important choice and we should make sure that our consciousness is adequately prepared to transmit the teaching of Yoga to others. We ought to be patient and wait until we have learned enough and possess enough knowledge before we begin teaching others. This is true in any field or profession, but especially as it concerns the teaching of Yoga and meditation. If we are only interested in gaining enough information to teach a basic asana class, then we need not wait until we have reached a satisfactory degree of Spiritual attainment. However, if we wish to teach pranayama, meditation, mantra, and philosophy, we should have already experienced the states of consciousness that we are teaching others about so that we may properly guide them.

We need not be fully Enlightened Gurus to begin teaching others meditation and Yoga philosophy, but we should be emotionally and Spiritually mature enough to teach in a responsible and sophisticated way so that our students will derive benefit. Otherwise, it is the blind leading the blind. A good way to know if we are ready to begin teaching and guiding others is to simply ask our Guru, if we have one. He or she will be able to judge whether or not we are ready. If we are part of a lineage, our Guru may decide to ordain us to consecrate our role as a representative of the Guru and his or her teachings. I was ordained by my Guru on July 5, 2012 and was told to begin teaching. I then had to wait another year until I had my Guru's blessing to begin initiating others into Kriya Yoga. I had already been studying with my Guru for five years before I was ordained and had been practicing Yoga and meditation for five years prior to meeting him. These things take time. We should not rush into Spiritual teaching out of an egotistical desire to impress others or to attract a following of students. Also, it is important to understand that many yogis choose not to teach and they quietly go about their Spiritual business behind the scenes. It requires a certain skill set to be a good teacher and many yogis do not possess this skill set. There is nothing wrong with practicing Yoga and meditation privately and choosing not to share knowledge with others. If we do decide to teach, it should be because we feel called to do so.

6 BELIEFS

"Don't be a believer, be a knower."
-Roy Eugene Davis

The belief system or religious affiliation that we choose to adopt indicates our level of emotional and Spiritual maturity. As yogis, it is recommended to leave behind antiquated and delusional beliefs that no longer serve our highest good and prevent us from maturing on our Spiritual growth path. Western yogis often have trouble undoing the brainwashing and programming that occurs in the Judeo-Christian churches of their upbringing. Some beliefs are so deeply ingrained into the minds of Western yogis that they are difficult to change and overcome.

I can vividly remember being ten years old and sitting in church and thinking that what the preacher was saying was intellectually flawed. I did not understand how a God that loves his children so much could send them to a lake of fire to burn eternally, and why only Southern Baptists were allowed into heaven. Even at the age of ten, I was able to use my discernment to deduce the fact that only a very small portion of the human population was Southern Baptist, and that the vast majority of humanity was hell-bound. It did not make sense to me why God would decide to punish all those people who did not know anything about Southern Baptist theology, and reward only those people who believed that the world was only seven thousand years old and created in a few days by a "jealous God." I was fortunate enough to have been born with the ability to think for myself and discern fact from fiction, but even so, it still took me a few years to shake off the conditioning that I had received until the age of sixteen when I made the conscious decision to stop attending my parents' church.

When I was fourteen, I began devouring Buddhist and Taoist texts and the writings of the American transcendentalists, Ralph Waldo Emerson and Henry David Thoreau. I knew from an early age that the dogma presented in my Christian church sounded much like the fairy tale stories I had read as a young child. The teachings of the East regarding reincarnation and Enlightenment made much more sense to me at the time, and I decided to pursue the path of Enlightenment from that point forward. The idea that I could become Christ-like, rather than merely singing hymns about him each Sunday was a profound step in the right direction. While I do not adhere to Buddhist and Taoist doctrine today, the basic ideas presented in the Taoist text the <u>Tao Te Ching</u> and the Zen writings of D.T. Suzuki left a lasting impression on me. Also, the writings of Thoreau and Emerson taught me that it was possible for people with a Christian upbringing to rise above the provincial beliefs that are taught in Christian churches. This gave me hope, and I knew it was possible to wrest myself free of the nonsensical views that I had been taught as a child.

Beliefs are not Spiritual; they are mental. So much of what people think is Spirituality, is actually just meaningless thoughts rumbling around in their heads. Religion is nothing more than mental stuff. Beliefs are not transformative and they do not change our state of consciousness. Beliefs do not affect us on a Spiritual level, only on a mental level. Yoga provides us with the opportunity to have direct experience of the Divine, rather than believing things that might or might not be true about the Divine. It is only through direct experience of the Ultimate Reality commonly referred to as God that we can hope to know anything about God. Reading things in religious texts regarding others' beliefs about God will not get us any closer to knowing God as God is. It is only through mystical, transcendent experience that we may know anything about God and the mysteries of the universe. Beliefs are composed of words, which are cognitive labels that we use to describe and understand the material world. Therefore, words can never describe something that is immaterial. Beliefs can never bring us any knowledge of the

Infinite because words cannot communicate that which is beyond verbal or written communication.

As our Spiritual unfoldment progresses, we realize that we are part and parcel of God and that separation from Ultimate Reality is impossible. Therefore, the Judeo-Christian belief that we are somehow separate from God and lesser than God must be discarded. There is only One Reality and we are a part of It and have never been separate from It, and we never will be separate from It. Samadhi provides the direct insight that there is only Oneness and that separation from God is an illusion.

The Western Christian belief that we are sinners and flawed from birth must also be discarded by any yogi intent on Spiritual Enlightenment. This view is counterproductive to those wishing to awaken Spiritually. If we believe that we are wretched sinners, then we are more likely to view ourselves in a negative manner. Christian guilt and unworthiness is highly self-defeating for our Spiritual unfoldment. Yoga philosophy states that we are inherently Divine and Infinite and that we only perform non-useful actions because our consciousness has become misidentified with maya. In deep states of mediation when our attention and awareness is no longer identified with our finite self, our Infinite, Divine nature can be unveiled and known.

I have asked many Christians, including members of my family who are practicing Southern Baptists, why they do not teach meditation in the Christian tradition. They have reported to me that Christians believe that by meditating, we are opening ourselves up to the possibility of demon possession. For those brought up fearing demons and demon possession, this may seem like a perfectly rational belief. However, in reality, this type of belief is completely ignorant. I am unaware of anyone in the history of the human race who has ever become possessed by demons from engaging in the practice of meditation. Too many Spiritual teachers stand idly by while these kinds of beliefs are propagated by the Spiritually ignorant masses and do nothing to refute them in the spirit of tolerance for the belief systems of others. We can tolerate the beliefs of others and at the same time attempt to educate people about the truth. We need not passively sit on the sidelines while people spread superstitious nonsense. It does not require from us a passionate emotional reaction. We can calmly educate the Spiritually ignorant people of the world in a kind and loving manner without judgment. In fact, this is what the great Spiritual Masters have always done throughout the ages.

Mr. Davis has the following to say as it concerns the promotion of false ideas:

> In our current era, in which the practical usefulness of rational thinking should be emphasized, some people who say they aspire to to spiritually enlightened still promote false ideas -- such as, "an independent intelligent satanic influence endowed with free will" tries to keep truth seekers in a state of ignorance. The meaning of the Hebrew word satan is "obstructor": not a personal, malicious influence. When a Greek translation of the Old Testament was done in the third century B.C.E., satan was changed to diabolus (much later to English devil). An endeavor to concentrate "evil" in a personalized form occurred before the 6th century B.C.E. in Persia (now Iran). The religious reformer, Zoroaster, believed that a Principle of Darkness was in a constant conflict with a Principle of Light. That idea was adopted by Hebrew religious teachers and later by Christians. To believe that malicious supernatural influences cause problems, pain, or personal or collective difficulties, or that "God allows it" indicates inability or reluctance to acknowledge what is true, undeveloped intellectual powers, and/or emotional immaturity.

There are not two forces competing with one another. Once one has experienced the Realization of Oneness, the idea of the epic battle of God versus satan seems ludicrous. In reality, there is only One Ultimate Reality. We experience suffering and misfortune because we are identified with the sufferer. Once this error in perception has been corrected, we no longer suffer. There still may be times when we experience misfortune and unfortunate events occur in our lives. Not everything is within our control. Not everything that happens is for our highest good, as some misguided Spiritual teachers would have us believe.

The idea that "everything happens for a reason" is simple minded. It assumes that all is predestined, and that God is producing all the events in our lives to lead us toward Spiritual growth. The universe is constantly unfolding itself and inventing itself and therefore is not predetermined. There is some Divine order underneath manifestation, but manifestation itself is somewhat chaotic and random and in constant creation. Furthermore, because we possess free will, we are co-creators of our reality. Things like war, famine, genocide, and corruption, do not happen because it is "God's will." Perhaps the universe was responsible for manifesting intelligent life, but that does not mean that the universe is responsible for manifesting everything that that same intelligent life decides to do with itself; otherwise, we would not truly be *intelligent* life. Therefore, the "reason" that things happen is simply due to a cause that created an effect and not because God magically pre-ordained it to happen. However, when something occurs that is not necessarily for our highest good, we still have the choice to react in a positive or negative way to events as they unfold. Also, as we grow Spiritually and elevate our consciousness, we find that we tend to attract more and more fortunate events into our lives. The universe is supportive of us, especially once we learn to cooperate with this support.

Another Spiritually immature belief that should be transcended is the idea that we need to be saved by a hero figure from the distant past to experience "eternal life." Once we realize that there is only One Reality and we are part of it, there is no need to ask a man that lived two thousand years ago to forgive us for our sins. Since we are a part of God, we can simply forgive ourselves. It is that simple. We need not wallow in guilt and shame for past misdeeds. We can choose to no longer identify with the false self that performed the non-useful actions in the past and move on. Through the process of daily superconscious meditation, we eliminate the elements of our human nature that desire to act in non-useful ways as we de-identify with the false self and all its flaws. This is the scientific process of Spiritual enhancement. A belief in a savior figure will not eliminate anger, greed, anxiety, fear, lust, and all of the other negative emotional states that get us into Spiritual trouble.

I can remember "getting saved" when I was very young in my church due to peer pressure, and thinking that I did not feel any different afterward. I was still the same confused and emotionally reactive child that I had always been. The only difference was that I *believed* I had been saved and that I was going to to go heaven when I died. It is common practice in many churches to encourage very young children to make the decision to "accept Jesus into their hearts" and become saved. Quite obviously, children are not developmentally ready to make a conscious decision such as this until well into their teens. The idea that parents would allow and encourage this type of major life decision to be made before the age at which children are even allowed to operate a motor vehicle is psychologically deranged.

We do not need to die before we can experience eternal life. It is happening right now. If the soul is eternal, then it has always been eternal and always will be eternal. It never had a beginning and it will never have an end. In the Western model, the eternal soul is somehow produced for the first time with the body and cannot experience eternal life until the body no longer exists. It is utterly astounding how many people believe this to be true.

Many early Christians known as the Gnostics professed beliefs in reincarnation and Enlightenment (Gnosis), but these beliefs were slowly replaced by the salvationist teachings of Paul. Paul's teachings were more conducive to uniting the Roman Empire under one state sponsored religion and Paul's' version of Christianity was also similar to Mithraism, which was very popular in Imperial Rome at that time.

Not much is known about Jesus Christ. All we really know about Jesus comes to us from the Gospels and the writings of Paul. Christ (christos) is a Greek word that is the translation of the Hebrew word messiah that meant one who would restore political control and free the Jews from Roman rule, and the word did not have any Spiritual connotations until much later. The first Gospel of Mark was written approximately thirty years after the death of Jesus. For anyone who has ever played the game of telephone, it becomes quite apparent that a thirty year game of telephone in ancient Israel would not lend itself to an accurate depiction of what may or may not have been said by Jesus during his lifetime thirty years before. The other Gospels were written much later and were based on Mark. Due to translations from Hebrew to Greek and then to other languages, mistranslations and errors, and additions by later scribes that skewed Jesus' words to fit their dogmatic interpretations, we really have no idea exactly what Jesus might have taught. Furthermore, the writings of Paul, a self-proclaimed apostle who never met Jesus, were based on an alleged mystical experience where Paul claimed he communicated with the spirit of Jesus. It is interesting that Christians denounce the channeled teachings found in all other religions, but place all of their blind faith in the channeled teachings of Paul of Tarsus.

Some of the Gnostic Gospels read more like Eastern philosophy, especially the Gospel of Thomas, and do not mention a salvationist theology. These texts were removed from official canon because they did not fit the dogmatic framework that Rome was attempting to construct with its version of the Bible. Paul's version of Christianity is based upon an apocalyptic theology. A belief in reincarnation eliminates the fear of a coming apocalypse. However, according to the New Testament, we should live in constant fear of a coming apocalypse and repent for our sins by accepting Jesus into our hearts. The belief in a one-lifetime model was advantageous for Imperial Rome. Combined with the perpetual fear of a coming Armageddon, Rome used the belief in a single incarnation as a way to control unruly, disparate populations. When we believe that the world is coming to an end soon, we are not very motivated to improve current political and economic conditions or overthrow despotic regimes. Likewise, if we believe that we only live once and that we will live in paradise as soon as we are dead, there is not much point in trying to make the world a better place to live in because we think we only have to come here once for a brief time, and then we get to leave and live in an eternal paradise. Rather than trying to create a heaven on Earth, we become content with the idea that Earth is supposed to be dreadful and we are going to live in eternal peace when we die anyway so there is really no point in improving Earthly conditions. We can see how these types of beliefs would have served an empire bent on global domination like Rome. The more Enlightened beliefs of Christian Gnosticism were replaced by this oppressive, apocalyptic, salvationist brand of Christianity that still predominates in today's world. It is the Spiritually immature belief in a coming apocalypse that has prevented humanity from making positive changes that would improve current conditions on Earth for the future generations of souls who will incarnate here.

Another Spiritually immature belief found within the Western Judeo-Christian system is the idea of original sin. This belief states that because Eve sinned in the Garden of Eden, we are all sinners and we must all bear her burden. Mr. Davis explains it as follows:

> The idea that suffering or dying could please a god is preserved in a widely promulgated Christian doctrine: the crucifixion of Jesus is said to atone for the sins or mistakes of others. Not only personal faults, also the lingering taint of the "original sin" that was said to have been committed by the mythical Eve that all humans are said to have transmitted to them when they are born. That no intelligent person should believe that to be true has not prevented many millions of people from professing it as a declaration of faith.

We are not inherently sinful and do not require saving. All that we require is to awaken from ego-consciousness through the stages of superconsciousness to complete Self and God-Realization. There is no one that can do that for us, and certainly not someone who lived two thousand years ago that we have no contact with.

We are currently living an eternal life. There is a part of our Being that is always "in heaven." We do not need to wait until we die to experience the Infinite. We have always been Infinite and always will be Infinite. We do not need to accept that someone died on a cross to experience the Infinite. We can go to heaven every day when we calm the fluctuations in our Being and experience the sacred stillness. There are higher astral and causal realms into which we may reincarnate that are preferable to this material dimension, but we need not wait until we are dead to experience heaven; it is right where we are, right now.

When the body dies, our astral/causal self, which includes the energetic body (pranamaya kosha), the mind (manomaya kosha), the intellect and individuality (vijnanamaya kosha), and the bliss sheath (anandamaya kosha), transport our soul to the astral plane (or causal plane if we are highly Spiritually advanced), and there we await our reincarnation back into form if we are so destined to reincarnate back into form. If we are more Spiritually advanced, we may remain in astral or causal planes as we continue our Spiritual unfoldment there. Also, it is possible to reincarnate on another physical planet, as our planet is far from the only planet in the universe to harbor intelligent life. Wherever our Being is reincarnated is due to our karma, and we are attracted into situations that match our particular karmic makeup.

Another common emotionally immature belief is the treatment of God as masculine or feminine. Since there is only One Reality, ascribing a gender to that One Reality is based on fantasy. Emotionally dependent people who treat God as a cosmic father or mother figure find solace and comfort in the idea. God as a father figure is common in many monotheistic religions the world over. As a response to this, simple minded people in the new age community have made it trendy to talk about Divine Mother and the Divine feminine as though assigning a feminine gender to God is any different or better. In Yogic traditions, the Divine masculine (Shiva) is usually associated with the unmanifest Infinite, while Divine feminine (Shakti) is associated with the manifest finite. However, these are arbitrary labels and are simply meant to help us understand two different aspects of the One Ultimate Reality. The goal of Yoga practice is to marry these two forces (Shiva and Shakti) alchemically in our Being resulting in Oneness. It is said that Shakti resides as Kundalini in the lower chakras and Shiva resides in the Sahasrara or crown chakra and that as we raise our Kundalini up the sushumna nadi to the crown, we bring together the material and Spiritual in Divine Union and experience Enlightenment.

It is best to avoid Spiritual trends and stay focused on our Spiritual awakening path. Many seekers make the mistake of becoming distracted by new age trends like channeling, chakra balancing, crystal healing, spirit guides, sacred geometry, astral projection, remote viewing, etc… While a few of these topics are fascinating and can be interesting to study, they will not bring us any closer to our goal of awakening through the stages of Spiritual evolution resulting in Self-Realization. Furthermore, many people waste inordinate amounts of time watching videos on the Internet related to trendy new age topics and think that they are growing Spiritually in doing so. In reality, they may have gathered more information in their head, but Spiritually, nothing has changed. It is easy to become distracted and confused on the Spiritual path and go side-tripping into the latest Spiritual fads, only to realize much later that not much has been gained internally from our intellectual studies. Our time is always better spent with our attention internalized probing the deep inner space of Ultimate Reality.

Another common mistake Western yogis continue to make is thinking that they need to adopt the deity worship, belief systems, customs, and rituals of Indian Hinduism in an attempt to appear more authentic and legitimate. There is no need for us to celebrate Hindu holidays such as Diwali or participate in ceremonies and rituals devoted to Shiva, Kali, Ganesha, or other Hindu deities. Likewise, there is no need for Westerners to travel to India to feel validated as yogis. No particular culture owns Yoga and meditation and anyone is free to practice the scientific methods of Yoga in any culture or nation of the world. If Yoga had not first appeared in India, it would have manifested somewhere else on the planet when the consciousness of the planet was ready. In fact, similar practices have emerged in cultures other than India. There is nothing about going to India that will accelerate our awakening process. There is nothing about performing fire ceremonies and chanting the names of Hindu gods that will lead to a quickening of our Spiritual unfoldment. Fire ceremonies and Sanskrit chanting can be Spiritually beneficial, but we should not feel obligated to participate in these activities in an effort to feel more legitimate as yogis. If we do decide to participate in Hindu rituals, it should be done as preparation for meditation. I often chant in Sanskrit as a prelude to my meditations and I find it beneficial.

Yoga is Spiritual science; it is not a religion. This is especially true in the West where it has largely been stripped of its religious encumbrances. The Yoga Sutras provides a step by step process by which we can unveil our true essence of Being, Unbounded Infinite Consciousness. This step by step process does not require us to have any particular belief system. The methods of asana, pranayama, pratyahara, dharana, and dhyana, if practiced correctly and repeatedly, will lead to Samadhi or Oneness Consciousness. Patanjali has given us a simple recipe for Enlightenment. We need not believe in a particular god or goddess, belong to a religious organization, or attend a specific church. All that is necessary is discipline, practice, and patience. Even beliefs about reincarnation, Kundalini, and astral and causal realms are entirely unnecessary for the practice of Yoga. Discipline, practice, and patience.

7 SAMPLE MEDITATION ROUTINE

Preliminary Kriya Yoga Meditation Routine

The following is a sample meditation routine for anyone interested in a simple, yet profound routine that, with diligent practice, will result in superconsciousness. These techniques are especially recommended for seekers interested in Kriya Yoga initiation. One should practice these techniques daily for a few months leading up to initiation to prepare the brain and nervous system for the more advanced Kriya techniques learned during the initiation. I have taught these practices to hundreds of people. I have found that those who commit to the routine and do it with discipline on a daily basis experience great benefit. However, the vast majority try the routine a few times, claim that it is not working, and give up. In order for any Spiritual practices to bear fruit, one must be fully devoted and practice with sincerity and patience. Expecting immediate results and instant gratification is a sign of Spiritual immaturity. It must be understood that it is the ego that craves instant gratification, and it is the ego that we are attempting to transcend by engaging in a disciplined meditation practice.

Sit in a comfortable, upright seated position, either in a chair or on the floor if that is appropriate for your body and degree of flexibility. There is no need to sit in half lotus or full lotus. Find a comfortable posture that works for you. If you find that doing some gentle asanas before sitting to meditate is beneficial then practice for 10-30 minutes in a meditative mood before you sit. If you are seated in a chair, make sure that your back is not touching the chair. Allow for one or two centimeters of space between your back and the chair and never let your head rest on anything, as this might lead to sleepiness or a lapse of attention.

Be fully present and alert. Do not allow attention to wander. Take a few deep breaths in and out. With each exhale, allow your shoulders to fully relax down the back. Sit with your attention and awareness in the forehead and upper brain. Doing so promotes the ability to focus and concentrate and also improves will power over time.

When you are settled, you can begin doing pranayama. Pranayama is meant to liberate the free flow of prana in the energetic body and also to balance this flow. We can also use pranayama to encourage the flow of prana upward in the sushumna nadi, or central energetic channel toward the higher chakras. This removes identification with our lower chakras and false self, and draws our attention and awareness to the higher Self.

The first pranayama technique is known as Nadi Shodhana, or alternate nostril breathing. Start by placing your right thumb on your right nostril and inhale through the left nostril. Next, close the left nostril with your right index finger and exhale through the right nostril. Leave your finger in place and inhale through the right nostril, place your thumb on the right nostril and exhale through the left nostril. This is considered one round of Nadi Shodhana. Our inhales and exhales should be of equal duration. Each breath should be long and slow, allowing for controlled and calm respiration. Twelve rounds of Nadi Shodhana is sufficient.

In order to count rounds of Nadi Shodhana, we can use our left hand. We have three pads on each finger. If we use our left thumb and start on the index finger, count three, and move toward the pinky counting three on each finger, we can count twelve total pads. Or, if you prefer to use mala beads, that is fine as well.

Following Nadi Shodhana, sit in the silence and enjoy the after effects of pranayama for a minute before you start the next technique. Notice that after you do pranayama your breath is more subtle and refined and less forceful. You may notice a relationship or correlation between the softness of your breath and the calmness of your mind. When you sit in the after effects poise of pranayama, notice any changes that might have occurred, physiologically and mentally. In Yogic texts, including the Yoga Sutras, the breathless state is mentioned. This is a state where the breath may temporarily cease and there is a tranquil silence and stillness in the body and mind. This is not a forceful holding of the breath, but rather a natural condition that may occur after pranayama or anytime during meditation. It should be observed objectively like any and all sensations or perceptions during meditation. Do not worry, your body will breathe again when it is ready.

After twelve rounds of Nadi Shodhana, in this particular routine, comes Sushumna Pranayama. Bring your attention and awareness to the spine. Imagine that there is a thin tube that runs through the physical spine the size of a straw. This "energetic spine" is known as the Sushumna Nadi. Now, imagine a small white light the size of a golf ball at the very base of your spine or the muladhara chakra. Allow it to hover there for a few moments while you begin your visualization. With your inhalation, gently draw the light up the astral spine, or Sushumna, and pull the current of energy over the back of the head, over the top of the head and into the Spiritual eye center or ajna chakra. Pause here for two seconds or so holding the breath, and then release the light back over the top of the head down the spine and allow it to rest at the base of the spine. Repeat this procedure twelve times. Breathing should be slow and inhales and exhales should be of equal duration. Afterward, sit in the deep silence for a minute or so and enjoy the par avastha, or after effects poise of pranayama. If you have difficulty pulling the current up the spine over the head, you can tilt your head forward slightly, dipping your chin. This declines the angle at which prana must travel over the head. There is a tendency for prana to become "stuck" around the shoulders and neck. With practice, prana will flow freely.

Following pranayama, you may decide to simply stay fully present in the stillness if you are in a relatively thought-free state of clear awareness. However, if you begin having thoughts, you should use the mantra "So-Hum." There are several different ways to use a mantra, but I suggest simply repeating the mantra over and over again silently in your head. Some teachers recommend linking the So with the inhale and Hum with the exhale, but I find that doing so keeps our attention too involved with the body and its processes and negates our attempts to transcend body identification. Therefore, simply repeat So Hum over and over in your head at a steady pace. You can experiment with the pacing of the mantra until you find a pace that works for you.

We use the mantra until we experience a clear, thought-free state, and we set the mantra aside for a while until we need it again. It is an organic process as we use the mantra to focus when we need it, and set it aside when we do not. Each time we return to the mantra, it should be done with the least amount of effort possible so that the process feels completely natural and effortless. You should use the mantra off and on for fifteen to twenty minutes to allow for longer and longer periods of tranquil silence. Five or ten minutes with a mantra is not enough for most people to silence the mind and experience superconsciousness.

During the final minute or so of meditation, set the mantra aside if you are using it and simply rest in the stillness as the objective observer or silent witness. Any time you have thoughts during the entire meditation process, simply ignore them and return your attention and awareness to your forehead and to the techniques being used. Do not participate in thoughts or react to memories, emotions, desires, or perceptions. Observe and detach. During the final minute when you are not using a technique, simply sit in the stillness and witness anything that comes up with dispassionate objectivity without the need to return awareness to a technique.

At the very end of your meditation, radiate loving kindness and compassionate goodwill out to all sentient beings everywhere and wish for them their highest good. In the Tibetan tradition, this is known as metta meditation. You can do this for as long as you would like, but devote at least a minute at the end of each session. It is very important to remember that you are not just meditating for your own benefit, but for the benefit of everyone, everywhere.

If you would like to chant Om out loud three times at the end of your session, it is a good idea. Chanting Om vibrates our entire body and Being with a Divine frequency. It is similar to plucking a dusty guitar string and watching the dust vibrate off of the string, cleaning the string and preparing it for further use. We can think of chanting in the same manner. We can visualize the Sushumna Nadi as the "guitar string" that we wish to vibrate and purify as we chant.

Below is a list of the meditation techniques in the routine for the sake of clarity:

Asana
-sit in a comfortable, upright seated position
-take a few deep breaths and bring your attention and awareness to your forehead and upper brain
Pranayama
-do Nadi Shodhana Pranayama 12 times
-sit in the after effects for one minute
-do Sushumna Pranayama 12 times
-sit in the after effects for one minute
Pratyahara/Dharana/Dhyana
-use the mantra So-Hum as needed for 15-20 minutes and enjoy the periods of thought-free awareness that occur in between the use of the mantra, possibly resulting in superconsciousness
-sit as the silent witness without using any techniques for one minute
-radiate compassionate goodwill and loving kindness to all sentient beings everywhere and wish for them their highest good for as long as you would like
-chant Om out loud 3 times
-conclude

You can use this routine once a day or twice a day. The entire routine lasts about thirty minutes. It is best to meditate first thing in the morning and again in the evening or before you go to bed. You will experience optimal results if you follow wholesome, healthy lifestyle regimens in addition to the daily practices. You may use a timer or clock in the beginning, but with practice, you will have a sense of how much time has transpired and will no longer rely on a timer or clock. Make sure that the area where you practice is clean, dark, and as noise-free as possible. You may wish to read inspirational material following your practice or simply go about your normal duties and activities. However, allow thirty minutes after your session to assimilate superconscious influences into the body and brain before you begin working or performing necessary duties. You can spend this time doing a short asana practice, chanting, reading, or even napping.

Do not become frustrated if you do not have positive results right away. You may need several months using this routine to become proficient at doing the techniques and calming the mind. If your desire to experience your true nature is sincere, then your commitment and devotion to meditation will follow. I have experimented over the years with many meditation techniques and routines and I have found this particular routine to be highly effective in eliciting superconscious states. None of these methods are my own invention. All of them have been used successfully by yogis for hundreds, if not thousands, of years.

If you have more time to devote to meditation, then you may extend your time with the mantra and/or sitting in the deep silence after pranayama. After a few months meditating for thirty minutes, you may prolong your sessions deciding to meditate for forty five minutes to an hour. Even if you choose to continue with a duration of thirty minutes, perhaps once a month or so, you should try meditating for an hour to experience the difference in longer sessions. Longer sessions provide us with the opportunity to dive deeper into the Infinite and gain insight into the nature of Ultimate Reality.

ABOUT THE AUTHOR

Christopher Sartain currently lives in Chile with his wife, Carolina. He is a Yoga and meditation instructor in the tradition of Kriya Yoga. Christopher was ordained a teacher in the tradition by Roy Eugene Davis on July 5, 2012. He has a Bachelors degree in Political Science, a Masters degree in Education, and a Specialists degree in Gifted and Talented Education. Christopher and his wife offer Yoga teacher trainings, retreats, and workshops in Chile and the United States.
Contact information:
chrissartain@gmail.com
www.vinyasayogachile.cl

Printed in Great Britain
by Amazon

79273090R00061